Ferris Wheel:

Life and Times of

the "Doc"

An Autobiographical Narrative

By

"Doc" Ferris

Published by Sarah Book Publishing
(A subsidiary of Litewill Holdings, LLC)
www.sarahbookpublishing.com

85 Industrial Drive Brownsville, TX 78521

ISBN: 978-1-61456-180-4

First Edition: June 2014

Book Cover Design: Sarah Book Publishing

www.sarahbookpublishing.com

Printed in the United States of America

The Story Begins...

I don't know why I've lived this long. Perhaps it's because I was born on February 29, 1928, and can claim only 21 actual birthdays. My family put on a heck of a surprise 21st birthday party for me. It actually caught me by surprise, and when I recovered from the shock, I realized how thankful I was for this celebration of love and friendship. Friends from Corpus Christi flew down for the surprise event. Everyone was laughing, talking and remembering how their lives were connected to each other through their friendship with my wife Sarah and me.

It all began some 40 weeks before February 29, 1928, with a twinkle in my parents' eyes. Nine months later I arrived at Breckenridge Hospital in Austin, Texas.

Wally Prior of Longhorn fame was born on the same day in Austin, but Mom won the First Baby of the Leap Year award because we came in first!

Mom was legally known as Frances Dean White. She was born in Monett, Missouri, on November 21, 1905, to Franklin D. White and Lulu Mildred Hawn. Franklin was a railroader in charge of the U.S. Mail on the M K & T. He died a hero at age 36, attempting to rescue his daughter Mildred and her friend, Clara Holland, when they wandered inadvertently into deep water at a picnic on the White River in Arkansas. Franklin was not a swimmer but went in after them, and all three were drowned. He was the grandfather I never met. He was posthumously awarded a Carnegie Medal for Heroism with some benefit to my grandmother, who now had two children to raise, my mother and her younger brother, David Lawrence White.

My grandmother, Lulu, known to me as Gama (Gamaw), moved to Austin, Texas, where she supported her family as a teacher at the State Institute for the Blind. With scholarship help, she sent her son to Schreiner Institute in Kerrville, Texas, where he studied pre-med and two years later entered Baylor Medical School in Dallas, Texas.

I remember my first long automobile trip to Dallas for Uncle David's graduation in 1933. It was a long trip because from Dallas, we went on to Arkansas, to visit Gama's brother and sister-in-law, Uncle Jim and Aunt Jo Hawn, in Fayetteville, and her sister Aunt Kate and Uncle Byron Brogdon, in Springdale.

Uncle Byron was an apple grower, and I vividly remember my first taste of real fermented apple cider. Driving up and down the rows of apple trees with Uncle Byron planted a seed in my mind that grew to find me in the avocation of citrus farming later in my professional life.

When I worked our orchards and drove up and down those rows of grapefruit and orange trees, I would often think of my days with Uncle Byron. I thought of him again when I was in basic training at Fort Lee, Virginia, as another soldier and I scouted the "enemy". We hid behind apple treetops, perched on the roof of an old tractor shed.

I'll have a great deal more to say about Gama and Uncle David later as they both had a profound influence on my life.

During my early childhood in Austin, we lived at 3110 Helm Street, in a simple, small frame home. I can remember my father coming home for lunch while the radio was playing music by W. Leo Daniel and his Country Doughboys band. Daniel later became Governor of Texas.

The country was deep into the Great Depression. Times were hard and I remember very poor people knocking on our back door to ask for something to eat. My mother always accommodated them. Dad was Advertising Manager for Papa's Department Store, and with his breakthrough talent in the promotion of newspaper advertising, S. Ferris Sons was a thriving business in a sea of disaster and unemployment. Dad was later to be a founder and President of the Austin Ad Club.

One of my most unpleasant memories of our life on Helm Street was the day our stove exploded in my mother's face when she was attempting to light the oven. I was playing on the floor in the living room in direct view of the event. She screamed and then cried out in pain and that was my first memory of an accident involving injury. Her face, hair, arms and hands were flash burned and I still remember the odor of singed hair and burnt flesh. My later years at Parkland Hospital in Dallas, as a surgery resident, always brought back those memories as we cared for so many badly burned people.

Life on Helm Street was significant for another future episode in my life. Our next-door neighbors, George and Mal McCulley, became fast friends with my parents. Mr. McCulley was working on his PhD at the University of Texas. My main interest was their two young sons, George Billy and Jimmy; one older and one younger than me. Our mothers grew close in friendship, and we three boys played well together with only a year's difference in age between the three of us.

George McCulley, PhD, eventually became the Registrar at Texas A&I College in Kingsville, Texas, located 40 miles west of Corpus Christi. After our family moved to Corpus Christi in 1937, it became a tradition for me to spend every Halloween holiday with the McCulley boys in Kingsville. How I loved those visits! We were nighttime pranksters and daytime players on the A & I Javelina football field. It was a real treat for sandlot players to find themselves in a real college stadium!

Mom was a Daughter of the American Revolution so I feel very secure in my American heritage. Now follows the hybridization and the "strengthening of America". Saadi Ferris (Papa Ferris to me) and Sophia Shipley (Mama Ferris to me) arrived at Ellis Island at different times. Sophia went to Nebraska with her family, and Saadi went to Manor, in the Austin area. At some point the two had met, and it wasn't long until the absence of Sophia prompted Saadi to sojourn to Nebraska, where he convinced the 16-year-old girl of his dreams to elope with him to Austin, where they settled to spend their lives and raise their family.

From their early life of peddling notions made by Sophia, they were able to gain the confidence of the community and eventually secure a loan from the Austin National Bank to open a small store on East 6th Street. As their family and their business grew, they were able to move across the street and open a much larger workingman's department store that catered to the rural and lower income folks struggling to survive the Great Depression.

Papa's astute business decisions during these trying times actually resulted in the accumulation of enough wealth to stop the run on the Austin National Bank. On that dark day of the bank moratorium in the early thirties, panicky customers were lined up to withdraw their money when Papa stepped forward and made a huge deposit. W.H. Folts, the bank's President was shocked and asked Papa if he knew what he was doing. Papa's response was, "You helped me start my business with a $2,500 good faith loan. Why shouldn't I help you?"

Mama and Papa's stately home still stands on 15th Street, in the shadow of the Capitol. My cousins and I spent many happy hours there. Sometimes these hours were a little less than happy for Papa. I can remember him calling out, "Mama! Can't you do something about these rowdy kids?"

I wasn't aware that we were that bad. Reality came in the 2nd grade at St. Mary's school when my Mother and Aunt Anna were asked to return my cousin, Jimmy Ferris, and me to Newman School where we had started first grade. Apparently we were the cause of general disturbances such as jumping in and out of windows and pulling a few pigtails. Sister Superior said no more St. Mary's for the Ferris cousins!

My two favorite playmates were my two first cousins, Johnny Booth and Jimmy. Johnny was the son of my Aunt Bertha Ferris, my dad's only sister, who was married to John Booth. Jimmy Ferris belonged to Uncle Ike (George) and Aunt Anna.

I loved to go to Aunt Anna's home because she understood kids and provided lots of freedom and goodies for us. I loved that my two older cousins, Teresa and Toots (Mary Lucille) were my first exposure to the ways of early teenage girls. Teresa played great songs on the piano and Toots seemed so grown-up. Those two older cousins were my first exposure to the ways of early teenage girls and I loved it. The baby of the household was Saadi, named in honor of Papa Ferris, and he and I stay in contact to this day. Saadi and his wife, Bobbie Jeanne Moore, live in Georgetown, Texas, where he retired after many years as a lawman. Saadi tells me that I am the patriarch of our generation since Teresa Ferris Lyon recently passed away. She lived in New York and often corresponded with Sarah and me. From her letters and the stories of her life, I truly believe she was a saintly woman. Her daughter Sheila Barnhart lives in Austin and is married to Mike Barnhart.

Mama Ferris was something else! A tiny, energetic woman, who would rise at 4 a.m. on the days she cooked one of her grand Lebanese dinners that delighted the palates of the entire family. After an aperitif of Anise, there was kibbe, mesche, grape leaves and yellow squash stuffed with rice and lamb as well as taboullie, hummus and baklava for dessert. I can still smell and taste that food in my fondest dreams.

Mama Ferris was born and raised in B'Sharri, a town nestled in the mountains and among the gorgeous Cedars of Lebanon. Her family name was Rahme. One of her playmates and cousins was Kahlil Gibran, author of *The Prophet* and many other literary works. She and Papa maintained a lifelong relationship with Gibran and would get together with him at a Lebanese restaurant in Brooklyn during their buying trips to New York.

Papa Ferris' brother, Rizcallah Elias Zeinoun, came to this country for a while but did not seem to like it here and returned to Lebanon. He did have two sons who came here and stayed.

Elias Ferris was the older son. With Papa's help, he established the Ferris Drug Store on East 6th Street, just a few doors east of the department store. Elias adored Papa because Papa brought him from Lebanon and provided support in establishing his business. Papa counseled him to establish his home in one of Austin's better neighborhoods and instructed him in matters of integrity and good business management. Elias ultimately owned three drug stores in Austin.

Anthony Rizcallah Ferris, the younger brother, was a language professor at the University of Texas. He translated many of Gibran's works from Arabic into English, the most notable of which was *The Prophet*. Anthony was also quite musical and played the lute. His work is featured in the Institute of Texan Culture at the Hemisfair in San Antonio in the Lebanese section.

Anthony eventually married Carmen Kazen from Laredo, and they had one son, Anthony P. Ferris, best known as Curly. Sarah and I recently met Curly when we visited the Shia family in Austin. Claire arranged a grand Lebanese dinner for us with Curly and Richard as special guests. We learned that Curly finished high school at age 15, college at age 17, and law school at age 19! He had to wait a year and a half to take the bar exam until he reached the minimum age of 21. He was truly an engaging dinner guest. After Anthony passed away, his widow Carmen visited us in the Rio Grande Valley on her trips for the State school system. She was a delightful and warm-hearted woman.

Sarah and I visited Elias and his wife, Rose, on many of our trips to Austin. We loved to sit with them and hear many stories about our family here and the ancestors in Lebanon. My old classmate and dear friend, Dr. Grover Bynum, a retired internist from Austin, would occasionally accompany me on my visits to

Rose and Elias and seemed to enjoy their stories of Old Austin, as much as I did. They had two sons, Richard and Jimmy. Richard and I visit from time to time about family lineage. Jimmy and his family live in Baytown, Texas.

Two of our closest friends in Austin, whom we dearly love, are a second-generation Lebanese family, George and Claire Shia. George is a practicing orthodontist, and Claire is a homemaker mother of six beautiful daughters, one of whom, Ramona, remains at home with them because of her health. Sadly, they lost their only son Gregory at the age of eight. With broken hearts, but a tremendous amount of faith in God's wisdom and goodness, they begin each day with Holy Mass and revel in the beauty of their daughters' families and grandchildren. We are so inspired by their example and friendship. They drove from Austin to our last family reunion in New Braunfels to meet some of our children and have lunch with us. We were joined by Dr. Jim McCutchon, from Corpus Christi, who frequently graces our reunions with his presence to the delight of all the family. Jim was married to my sister Jeanne who died from breast cancer in 1996. Jim and I have remained close for many years and still call each other "Bro". We were classmates at Tulane Medical School in the Class of 1953. We each married our sweethearts within 4 days' time and my mother lost her only son and daughter within one week. However, she gained two of the most wonderful children that any mother-in-law could possibly have!

Both weddings were at the beautiful Corpus Christi Cathedral, Jimmy and Jeanne on June 8, with a Nuptial Mass, and Sarah and I on June 12, 1953, with a more traditional mixed marriage wedding. Sarah was not Catholic in name on our wedding day, but she most certainly was in spirit. She had a wonderful counselor and instructor in the person of Father Anthony Goegele. During my senior year in medical school and her first year of school teaching at Fischer Elementary in Corpus Christi, Father Anthony instructed her in the Catholic faith. He wisely counseled her to postpone her Baptism until after the wedding to show respect for her parents and grandparents who were very devout Methodists in order to have them be more comfortable with a traditional mixed marriage ceremony. Jimmy and I were recently together at the 59th reunion of our Tulane Medical School Class of 1953. We met at The Gulf Hills Resort in Ocean Springs, Mississippi. Eighteen of our classmates showed up and the camaraderie was as good as it gets for a group of octogenarians! We are the only Medical Class in Tulane's history that has met for so long on an annual basis. Aging, of course, will naturally terminate this nostalgic tradition, but until it does, "Lassais les bons temps rouleau" – translation "Let the good times roll"!

After Uncle David graduated from Baylor Medical School, he went to New York City for his internship. I remember seeing him off at the train station with all of the family, and we were there again one year later for his return home. It was a big deal in those days to go to a prestigious New York hospital and come back to practice your skills among the folks who knew you from childhood!

My uncle, David L. White, M.D., chose to settle in San Marcos, just 30 miles south of Austin, where he associated with an older physician, Dr. Williams, in a general practice. In those days country doctors took care of every imaginable situation other than the most obvious disasters that required transfer to a major medical center. He became proficient in urgent surgery, Obstetrics, Pediatrics and general emergencies.

I visited his office many times, talked with his nurses, and accompanied him on house calls as far away as Luling, Bastrop and Wimberley. I saw the deep appreciation folks had for his care and how energizing his work seemed to be as he faced new and challenging situations almost daily.

I would later contrast that with my father's retail clothing business and the choice for me was quite clear.

8

I don't mean that my father's calling was any less important. After all, people needed to be clothed, and the wise merchant learns how to perform that service in an efficient and economical manner, just as Papa Ferris had done in the Great Depression.

It was in my Uncle's medical office that I first learned I was colorblind. One of his nurses became suspicious and challenged me with a set of Ishihara test plates, a set of multicolored circles containing numbers or letters. Persons with normal color vision see one number and colorblind people see a different number or no number at all. I failed and lost any chance to fulfill my desire to fly at night, captain a ship, go to the Naval Academy. One has to be able to distinguish red from green at night to qualify for any of those licenses.

There were other attractions about Uncle David's life that fascinated me. He always seemed to find time for adventure in his life such as hunting, fishing, flying and traveling. My dad and mother, on the other hand, spent a great many weekends at the store surviving. Their loving sacrifices enabled my sister and me to choose different paths and go to the very best schools.

Through my mother, Uncle David befriended the Gallagher family in Clarkwood, a small farming community west of Corpus Christi. Daddy Jack Gallagher had a hunting lease in the South Texas brush country somewhere near the town of Alice. Uncle David asked me to join a hunting party. They were planning to camp out in the brush and do some walking and rattling for a three-day deer hunt. It was my first big hunt and I was excited. Daddy Jack took me under his wing on the first morning out, and we walked until he selected a place to rattle. Rattling consists of banging deer horns together simulating a buck fight. During the mating season, the ordinarily wary and cautious buck deer, tend to lose these survival qualities as their raging hormones sense the presence of the fertile females. They are territorial and the larger and more physically mature deer are quite intolerant of the younger and less experienced males. Some serious fights break out when a younger buck decides he is 'macho' enough to take on Big Daddy; thus the genesis of rattling to simulate a buck fight and draw out the dominant buck.

Walking hunters learn how to practice stealth, evaluate the landscape, find the wind direction and position themselves in such a way as to have an advantage. I had great teachers and I pursued perfection in that sport until my heart grew soft with age and I preferred to watch those beautiful animals. I taught my young sons to hunt and some of them, like Paul, taught me a few techniques!

During the early years of Uncle David's practice in San Marcos, Gama White was still living in Austin, and he often drove over to visit, go shopping, or take flying lessons. I always wanted to be at Gama's when Uncle David was coming. One afternoon he took me with him to a local airport for one of his flying lessons. The subject for that particular day was stall prevention and how to correct a resulting tailspin. I watched from the ground while he and his instructor performed several intentional stalls and successful tailspin corrections. I wanted to do that! I wanted to be like Uncle David!

In 1945, when I was in the Army Specialized Training Program at Texas A &M, my first flying lesson was pretty exciting. The instructor in the rear of the tandem seated Aeronca Cub let me taxi to the runway where we revved the engine for takeoff. Then, to my surprise, he told me to give it full throttle and keep it in the middle! What followed wasn't very pretty. That Cub veered from one side of the runway to the other as my heavy feet on the rudder pedals kept over-correcting. Finally, he took over to straighten us out and get us airborne. He then tested my resolve and fear factor by taking us to a sufficient altitude for a couple of stall-outs and tailspins. The emotions of falling in the stall with the earth spinning below, followed by comforting G forces as we pulled out,

10

made an exciting day for this neophyte pilot. I was so excited I called home to tell my folks of my newfound experience. Bad mistake! I needed supplemental funds from home to continue this adventure since it was not part of the ASTP program. I was quickly assured that funds would not be available for this newfound extracurricular activity. I rationalized my parents' decision by realizing that a colorblind person could never fly at night or by color control, or be able to have a class II or III certificate. My career as a pilot was over.

Gama, my maternal grandmother, had a tremendous influence on my life. About the time I was five or six years old, I was permitted to spend the night at her home on West 38th St., where she owned a classic Austin duplex, living in one half and renting the other half; as always, a very strong and self-sufficient widow.

Her home was very warm and cozy and I spent many hours there listening to her wisdom, eating her delicious waffles, learning to play cards and other games such as dominos and checkers, and listening to her favorite songs, such as "Home on the Range", and her stories of Will Rogers. She grieved openly when Rogers, an American icon, and his friend and pilot Wiley Post were killed while flying in Alaska. She was a strong Christian and faithful member of the Lutheran Church. I dearly loved being with her and as I look back on my time with her I realize that she was the epitome of the real American woman. She was a Daughter of the American Revolution and could trace her ancestry back to Colonial times from Scotch, Irish, English and German ancestry.

I loved and wanted to be with her so much, that one day, I must have been 5 or 6 years old, I left our home on Park Boulevard and began a journey to her home on West 38th, a distance of about 2 miles. I became lost in Pease Park, where a bread delivery driver recognized my plight and was able to get enough information from me or someone else to get me back home.

On another visit to Gama's, Uncle David drove up from San

Marcos, and brought me a baby Persian kitten. She was a beautiful light yellow, furry little ball. It was love at first sight. She was so cute and playful. Another early lesson about sadness in my life came when I jumped over a low hedge, not knowing the little kitty was on the other side, and my foot crushed her. She died quickly and I had a lesson in heartbreak.

Other early memories of life in Austin included Uncle Nick and Aunt Boling coming by in the evening in their Packard convertible for a drive around Austin, or a trip to Toonerville for the best hamburgers in Travis County. My parents loved evening drives and showing me the Capitol, which I called the "Kongkong", and the lighted tall bell towers so identified with early Austin.

My dad & mom loved to sing together on our evening rides. I still find myself singing those old favorites, especially when I'm traveling and away from the concerns of medical practice. "There's A Long, Long Trail a 'Winding'", "Let Me Call You Sweetheart", "School Days", "I Want a Girl Just Like The Girl Who Married Dear Old Dad". None of us had any singing talent but that didn't dampen our enthusiasm for song! Eighty years later I still love to sing my dad's old favorites and sweet Sarah tolerates it – possibly because she's lost a good bit of her hearing!

Our last few years in Austin, we lived at 600 Park Boulevard. We were on the northeast corner of the intersection with Barrow Avenue, just one block East of Duval Street. It was a beautiful neighborhood with Park Boulevard slowly descending to a lovely stone bridge over a lazy creek, then proceeding upward to meet Red River Street, forming a lazy U pattern, downhill and uphill with the creek at the bottom of the U. This sidewalk formed a perfect testing ground for our scooters and wagons to race down to the creek, from either end of Boulevard.

Two of my neighborhood playmates were the Sherwood brothers. Their dad made us a kite so large we had to have a grown person hold on to us in order to fly it. We were literally dragged along the ground. Another playmate was Winona Moorhead. I believe her father was the District Attorney for Travis County. All of us played together without a care in the world.

My little sister Frances Jeanne was born on August 6, 1933. When I was 8 years old, the Austin American Statesman published a picture of 3-year-old Frances Jeanne and me writing a letter to Santa Claus. The picture became a family memento, and we still have copies of it.

Apparently my dad was growing restless and dreaming of pursuing his own career in the business world. The next thing I knew I was on a trip to Corpus Christi, with my dad and Papa Ferris, to explore the possibility of opening a men's clothing store in the booming oil town.

The year was 1937. It must have been in the Spring, because I entered public school for the first time at Crosley Elementary in the Hillcrest neighborhood of Corpus Christi. I think I transitioned well, but I did miss the prayers and the nuns to whom I had become accustomed. I was to be there only a short time because in the Fall semester of the school year I found myself in the 4th grade at the Incarnate Word Academy, just half a block from my dad's new clothing store.

My new 4th grade teacher was Sister Ignatius, and she was just as tough as her name sounds. If one's penmanship wasn't close to the book, there was a severe rap on the knuckles with her ruler. Ouch! My mother complained and I hated it. I shouldn't have told her because I needed to learn to fight my own battles. But there she was, overprotecting me. Shades of the problems teachers are facing today! Abject cruelty and abuse is one thing, but a little hickory stick discipline never hurt, and probably helped, many a kid.

Anyway, life was proceeding well in Corpus Christi. Dad had opened John A. Ferris Fashions for Men, on the first floor of the

Nixon Building, a location buzzing with business and professional people. The area was known as The Hill because Corpus Christi's central business area was on two levels, the lower known as downtown. The main thoroughfare was Leopard Street, which divided the Plaza Hotel from the Nixon Building, located across from each other. My school, Incarnate Word Academy, occupied the entire second block of Leopard, except for its NE corner, the site of St. Patrick's Church, home of the Diocese of Corpus Christi, and its spiritual leader, Bishop Ledvina.

My 5th grade teacher was a happy little nun, Sister Aloysius, whose joy and smiling face were quite infectious. The school year passed quickly and uneventfully. Mom was happy to be in a different home on Ohio Street, looking after my little sister Jeanne, keeping an eye on me, and occasionally helping Dad at the store. She became involved in the Cub Scout movement and helped the Pack Mother teach budding scouts about leading honorable and productive lives. My neighborhood playmates were James Kuentsler, Neil Keeble and BB Ogden. Life was good!

Summer vacation meant a chance to go to San Marcos and spend time with Gama and Uncle David. The folks would put me on the train or the bus and I could make the trip alone. I loved those Summers in San Marcos.

Gama had sold her home in Austin and moved to San Marcos to be closer to Uncle David and keep house for him. I felt so at home with them and received lots of attention.

Sixth grade would be my last year at Incarnate Word Academy and the year I had my favorite teacher, Sister Benedict. She was stern, but fair, and very good at imparting knowledge to young minds. I understand now what the nuns knew about adolescence and puberty, and why there were no boys in seventh grade at IWA. Alas, I began to notice that the girls in my class were sort of special, and sort of pretty. One in particular attracted my attention with her long, straight sandy hair and her very beautiful face. I

14

imagined Jeanne Stewart would be my girlfriend, if I ever had a girlfriend, and I didn't, so it really didn't matter. Our mothers began to promote dancing lessons and occasional supervised parties to enhance our social skills. We boys weren't very good at it, but weren't supposed to be at that age. I also remember Patsy Stitt and Alice Kleberg from the King Ranch family. There were some really bright boys in that class, like Walter Henry Franks, Harry Plomarity, and Michael Meaney.

A major problem was about to occur that would separate me from that talented group of students. Most of us now found ourselves as seventh graders at a Benedictine high school for boys, the Corpus Christi College Academy. This school was located on Shell Road, a few miles outside of the city limits, and we rode a school bus to and from town. If we missed the bus, we trod to town or hitchhiked, whatever seemed the best plan at the time. Rural people who lived in the area recognized us as CCCA students and were very good about giving us a ride when we needed it.

The faculty at CCCA was composed of Benedictine Monks from the Abbey at Subiaco, Arkansas. Most were of German heritage and very fine disciplinarians. They had great insight into the ways of adolescent boys. They had firm rules for a happy life and always treated us fairly. Their credo expressed in Latin was "Ora et Labora", Pray and Work! My lasting impression was that they did that joyfully and set a wonderful example for us as teenagers.

I loved my mother very much and I've tried to understand the horror and pain she experienced when she witnessed the drowning of her father, her sister Mildred, and her sister's friend, Clara Holland. This emotional trauma, as I look back, was an experience from which she never recovered. I believe she became neurotically determined to never experience the loss of another loved one and operated in a mode of fear and overprotection.

I loved football and I was determined to play for the CCCA Cavaliers. When I reached the eighth grade, I went out for the football program run by Father Alcuin Kubis as head coach and his assistant Father Harold Heiman. Our school was small, so some of our younger candidates played as symbolic pass defenders during scrimmages with the older guys who were instructed to avoid serious contact. Harold Macha, a talented senior back, much bigger and faster than me, was keeping his eye on a pass and collided with me at full speed and laid me out cold. I thought I'd been hit by a freight train. It was about 2-3 minutes before I could take a breath. Some kind soul carried me home and presented me to my mother. Bad mistake! She entered her overprotective mode and the next day I was a late registrant at the Robert Driscoll Junior High School where there were no sophomores, juniors or seniors, and worst of all there was no eighth grade. Texas had just gone from an eleventh to a twelfth grade plan in order to be graduated from high school. CCCA held back my old class in the eighth grade; Driscoll moved their eighth graders to the ninth grade and had no eighth grade for me. I became an overnight ninth grader. I would never be in my old class again. When my mother decided I could return to CCCA, I was put in the 10th grade without the benefit of a full complement of high school math. My journey through pre-med and medical school was difficult wherever advanced math and the biological sciences crossed paths, and it seemed those intersections were quite frequent. Human brains are commonly known to have strengths and weaknesses, and I believe that math occupied a very small area of my cerebral geography, sort of like the U.S. and the state of Rhode Island! I was not deterred because I seemed to know that my forte would be patient care and not research. I feel super competent in my ability to relate to patients, to listen, to analyze, to communicate, to accurately diagnose and treat all but the most complex of disorders. I love doing that and working with various specialists to be sure I'm giving my patients the very best care available.

Writing this history has raised a totally new question in my mind that previously I never considered. When my mother was in her overprotective mode and made changes that significantly affected my future development, where was my dad? Did he have any masculine input into these nuances of adolescent development? I'll never know. Chances are he was "working at the store", a phrase too often heard in too many families. One thing I feel I do know is that well-balanced kids come from well-balanced families with interactive parents. Sounds like an alibi for any deficiencies I see in myself. Perhaps it is!

Scouting was a big part of my teenage years. As I mentioned earlier my mom started me off in the Cub Scouts with my den mother Mrs. Kuentsler, the mother of one of my playmates, James, whom I mentioned earlier. The Kuentsler family lived across Ohio Street from us so activities were easy to attend. Progress through the Cub program involved learning how to complete small projects and activities, particularly football. I really loved our Cub Scout football team. One day we were practicing in the front yard of Menger Elementary School where there was a flagpole in the middle of the main sidewalk. That sidewalk was more or less our goal line. In the huddle I was named a pass receiver and my job was to aim for the goal line where I could expect the arrival of a touchdown pass and I better not drop it. I performed my task full speed ahead, looking over my left shoulder as the ball floated beautifully into my waiting arms. CRASH!! Somehow that flagpole became an outstanding defensive back and the football and I crumbled to the ground. The next thing I knew I was standing at the front door of my home, and the coach was presenting me to my mother with a blood soaked head and a gash on the forehead. Funny, but I do not remember any more Cub Scout football games after that. Dr. Bickley, a family doctor in the Nixon building, sewed up my head, and I was spared any complications.

When I reached age 12, I met the requirements to become a

Tenderfoot Scout in Troop 23, a group of adolescent Catholic boys under the guidance of Scoutmaster Walter Franks, a genuinely good man. He was employed by Central Power and Light Company in the accounting department. His boss was W.D. Boone, another genuinely fine man, who was also very active in the Scouting movement. Mr. Franks was the father of one son and seven daughters, and Mr. Boone was the father of seven sons and one daughter. How I loved those two families and I spent lots of my growing up time in their respective homes.

My peer in the Boone family, and fellow 6th grader at IWA, was George Bannantine Boone. The worst news I could possibly imagine came to me the following Summer while in San Marcos. George had died from peritonitis complicating a ruptured appendix. I could not imagine such a thing!! How could one so young and so vibrant be taken away from this world and my friendship? I remember my parents trying to tell me about it over the phone. I was lucky to have had Gama and Uncle David to try and help me understand. It was my first experience with real grief. We were living in the pre-antibiotic days, so there was no weapon to fight bacterial peritonitis. I cannot help but believe that subconsciously, George's death was a subliminal factor in my decision to become a physician.

I loved the experience of scouting and as I progressed from Tenderfoot to Second-Class, to First class, to Star, to Life, and ultimately to Eagle, I learned that it was not just me accomplishing those goals, but my parents, my scoutmaster, my teachers, and my peers encouraging me to meet the goals and not quit until I arrived. I owe them all a great deal because it prepared me to meet my ultimate goals of marriage, family and a career of helping other people. My marriage has been a real blessing, my family has brought me great joy and I don't believe any physician could have relished his practice any more than I have. I have loved my interaction with patients in spite of a few bumps in the road. I had many patients that I dearly loved to see and who have brought me great joy and satisfaction to my life.. Whatever joy I have experienced flows also to my wife and family and strengthens the fiber that binds us one and all. They have also shared a few of the sorrows when things haven't gone so well, and these negative emotions can also be a binding force that strengthens family ties.

The most exciting event of my scouting years was the opportunity to go to Philmont, a large ranch donated to the scouting movement by Waite Phillips, of Phillips 66 fame. Located in northern New Mexico, the ranch had several different ecologies for a great variety of scenery and altitudes. We acclimated for a week at base camp where we learned New Mexico and ranch lore and became accustomed to the wonderful afternoon mountain rain showers that made our siestas cool and restful.

Our second week involved learning horsemanship and how to be a cowboy at Cimmaroncito, a Western ranch atmosphere that included care and respect for the animals and how to manage them on the trail. The third, and my favorite week, took us hiking to the higher altitudes and mountain forests where we discovered running streams, watched beavers building dams and small lakes, cooked our own meals, bathed in the streams, and rested our weary bodies in pup tents at night. We imagined all sorts of encounters with bears, wolves and mountain lions that never actually happened, but kept adrenaline-like excitement in our veins. We did come upon an old twin-engine aircraft that had crashed into the mountainside. This sight opened all sorts of speculation about the fate of the passengers and the crew, and how we would have handled such a situation. It helped an adolescent mind consider that one is not always in total control of one's destiny. Accidents happen and lives on this earth are in no way guaranteed. A subtle lesson about finding and getting about the business of one's chosen purpose as early as possible is a worthy accomplishment.

We finally returned to camp headquarters for final ceremonies with songs of patriotism, brotherhood, goodbyes and memories that would last a lifetime.

My last three years at CCCA were difficult for me for many reasons. I was ahead of my old class and the only students in the 10th grade were transfers from other schools. There was no progressive structure for stepwise learning, and my schedule was improvised based on what subjects were available. I endured a good bit of teasing and torment about being a mama's boy from upper classmen and my old classmates, which was painfully true. My best friend was Harry Stuth, and he was 2 years behind me, but quite mature and an "All South Texas Guard" on the football team. His friendship gave me some confidence and some stature. We remained close friends for a long time, and with his encouragement, I was back on the football team by my senior year, albeit as a 2nd string right tackle, behind Francis Phillipp, a boarding student from La Feria, Texas. Fate would have it that one day I would practice medicine in La Feria, and Francis would be my patient.

Francis still comes to see me for his aches and pains 66 years later, and we have a great relationship. His cousin, Albert Bauer, also from La Feria, was a year behind us and played first string guard. We had a great year opening against Martin High in Laredo, a team that was supposed to trounce us, and we won 13-7. I played in 4 quarters of that game and never thought I could be so pumped up with pride. *Corpus Christi Caller Times* sportswriters were shocked at our victory and gave us plenty of publicity. I was gaining confidence.

Francis and Albert both lived on family farms south of La Feria, married wonderful girls and raised beautiful families. Albert died of pancreatic cancer a few years ago, but with relentless faith in God, he fought the good fight and survived longer than any patient I've ever known with that dreaded malady. His widow, Joanie, a very happy and vivacious person, still comes to see me and revels in the lives of her children and grandchildren. Nearly all of those good German people were from parents who migrated to La Feria from the Gainesville and Munster areas of North Texas. Oddly again, my son, Christopher worked in Gainesville, and his two boys, Christopher and Logan, attended St. Mary's, the same Catholic school in which the La Feria settlers began their education.

The rest of our football season was quite good, and I played often, though not as much as I wanted because Francis was a stalwart player in our position. We won over Sinton, Aransas Pass, and St. Anthony's of San Antonio, but lost to Taft and Alice by narrow margins and Benavides 20–0. Benavides had many 200-plus pound linemen while we averaged about 160 pounds. One of those giants stepped on Larry Sullivan's stomach, and he had to stay in the hospital overnight. Overall we had a good year and I gained a great deal of self-confidence thanks to Coach Father Harold, Harry Stuth, and my teammates.

It was customary for the graduating seniors to play next year's varsity team at the end of their Spring training session. Alas! Our Senior Class had only twelve players, which meant eleven starters and one man on the bench. Our 12th Man, to quote an Aggie tradition, was Bill Loessberg. The real 12th Man of Aggie fame was Dr. Earl King Gill, of Corpus Christi, where he eventually practiced as an ear, nose, and throat specialist. I remember visiting him as a patient when I was a teenager. Returning to the "Great Game" between our Class of '45 and next year's varsity, we humbled them with a 2-0 victory when we tackled one of their ball carriers behind the goal line!

Before leaving Cavalier football in the 1944 season, I must mention our starting backfield of Johnny Golla and Frank Gamez, halfbacks; Pancho Gomez, fullback; and Nick "Short-arm" Ortiz, quarterback. Three of these players could run the 100-yard dash in just over 10 seconds and the fourth was only 1-1.5 seconds behind.

Golla scored 7 touchdowns against Aransas Pass with his broken field running. Nick's "short-arm" passes were deadly, and Pancho could get through the middle with lightning-like speed. It was a great year for me and the Cavaliers!

I want to go back now to junior high and the ninth grade at Robert Driscoll. At that time we were living in Saxet Heights, a subdivision in the western part of Corpus Christi. I was with an entirely different set of public school kids. My best friend there was Vincent Tarlton. His dad was a very prominent lawyer in Corpus Christi. His mom was quiet and retiring, but she always seemed to welcome me in their home. Vincent had an older sister known as Sissy, who was destined to marry George Farenthold. Sissy would ultimately run for Governor of Texas. She did not win that election, but she ran a spirited race. Vincent also had two brothers, one of whom died very young from the aspiration of a quarter. His other brother was Dudley, named after his father, and he was 2 to 3 years younger than Vincent. I never knew him well. I would run into Vincent again when I entered pre-med at Tulane University in New Orleans. At that time we did not have much in common and I do not think I have seen him since then.

At Driscoll High School, I was going to school with girls again, and this seemed strange after a year at the College Academy. I re-met Patsy Stitt, from the sixth grade at IWA, but we did not see much of each other. I thought the cutest girl in school was Vietta Brewer, a very pretty blonde with short hair. Unfortunately, she had a steady boyfriend and didn't know I existed.

I don't remember anything about my teachers or classes at Driscoll, which I thought contrasted with the excellent and intense instruction the priests gave us at CCCA. I really missed the prayers, going to Mass in the Chapel, pausing to say the Angelus at noon, and the feeling that the monks really cared about our souls and the quality of our future lives and families. I was so happy to return to CCCA in the Fall of 1941, but I did not realize how severely this dislocation would impact my future. Outwardly I thought it was cool to be a year ahead of my class and be graduated a year early. Inwardly, I wanted it to be "The Way It Was".

It was December 7, 1941, and Vincent Tarlton and I were playing "knee football" in the front yard of our home with a couple of neighborhood chums. We played on our knees because our front yard was too small to accommodate an upright game. It was still a rough game but not so far to tumble. I remember the next scene as if it happened 10 minutes ago. My dad opened the front door with a look of disbelief on his face and called out, "The Japanese bombed Pearl Harbor"!! Our involvement in World War II had begun! Our way of life and our Nation's very existence was placed at risk. President Roosevelt addressed a joint session of Congress on December 8, calling December 7, "a day that would live in infamy".

Uncle David left his practice to the older doctors in San Marcos and appeared at our home on December 9 on his way to volunteer for the Navy Medical Corps. The recruiting stations across the country were jammed with young and middle age men ready to defend our freedom with their fortunes and their lives. Women volunteered for the WAVES, the WAFS, and the WACS, and many went to work building ships and planes. Rationing of gasoline, strategic commodities, and other essential products went into effect as America rolled up her sleeves in the defense of our way of life. The prophecy of the Japanese admiral in command of the carrier fleet that attacked Pearl Harbor was about to come true when he mused, " I'm afraid we have awakened a sleeping giant!"

Uncle David was processed into the Navy and assigned to the Marines. We prayed hard for his safety and for the safety of all of our troops upon whom our way of life depended. Ultimately he and five other doctors went ashore as battalion surgeons for the Marines during the initial invasion of Guadalcanal. Only two of them survived.

I came home from school one afternoon, popped through the front door in my usual fashion to find Uncle David sitting in our living room. I was ecstatic! I crushed him with one bear hug after another. It was one of the most joyful days in my life. I prayed thankfully for his safety. He was with us and around San Marcos for a month or so and then went back to duty in the Pacific. He later developed some kind of tropical fever on that tour and came home to stay and get well. We owe that "greatest generation" so much.

Patriotism was alive and America put her shoulder to the wheel to defend our great country now formally at war with the Axis Powers of Japan, Germany and Italy. CCCA became somewhat military and certain days we wore army uniforms and drilled to cadence. Gas, meat and sugar rationing went into effect and highway travelers limited their speed to 35 mph to save precious fuel. Blackouts were practiced so potential enemy bombers and submarines could not see our cities at night. We knew that German submarines plied our Atlantic and Gulf coasts and that they took a terrible toll on supply ships headed to our troops in Europe. Patriotism surged through our blood as we envisioned living under any other form of government than the freedom for which our forefathers fought and died.

The Corpus Christi Naval Air Station was burgeoning with young aviator cadets to shore up our war effort. Auxiliary bases were established in Kingsville and Beeville, 40 and 50 miles to the west and north of the main air station. Nearby auxiliary fields, such as Cabiness and Cuddahy, were constructed by the Brown & Root Company to enhance pilot training.

John A. Ferris Fashions for Men was now in the Naval and Marine officer uniform business. Jake Stephens was in charge of this effort, and I was his assistant during the Summer break and after school. Jake was the leader of a local orchestra with the Big

Band sound of the 40's. We would travel to the various air bases and fields to market made-to-measure uniforms about two months ahead of graduation. The pilots looked really spiffy in their perfectly fitted Naval and Marine uniforms. I remember outfitting the handsome movie star, Tyrone Power, and George "Sonny" Franck, the All American halfback from the University of Minnesota. I was thrilled to receive an autographed action photo of Ensign Franck running with the football.

President George H.W. Bush also came through Corpus Christi, as the youngest cadet in the flying program, but I did not have the privilege of knowing him until many years later. After his torpedo bomber was hit and disabled by enemy fire, he ordered his two crew members to bail out. He never saw them again and said that the loss of those two men became the greatest sorrow in his life. Fortunately a nearby courageous American submarine captain and crew surfaced and rescued our future President before the pursuing Japanese powerboats could capture him.

The rest is history. Allied forces swept through North Africa and defeated the Desert Fox Rommel. Our troops crossed the Mediterranean and proceeded northward through Italy until that country surrendered, and its people hung Mussolini by his heels. Germany was reeling and being pummeled by American B17 bombers while Allied infantries advanced and the Russian Bear closed in from the east. Hitler retreated to Berchtesgaden with his mistress, Eva Braun, where he completed a suicide pact that would spare them the fury of an angry world.

The war in the Pacific was turning our way after the great battle of Midway essentially defeated the Japanese Navy. The culture of the Japanese soldier was to fight to the death since surrender was not an acceptable option. If not killed in battle, the act of Hari Kiri was the only honorable solution. Japan occupied many Pacific Islands and began the task of constructing tunnels and caves from which to defend their Empire unto death.

It was on the Island of Kumashima, July 2, 1945, just 29 days before the war ended, that Jim McCutchon's brother, Edward Davis McCutchon, Jr. gave his life to preserve our way of life. His Marine unit's mission was to destroy a strategic radio transmitter, a small cog in the wheel of war, but a giant sacrifice for this man and his heartbroken family. Their ultimate and enormous sacrifice was a measure of the cost of freedom! Edward had fought and survived the terrible battle of Okinawa and did not deter from his assignment at Kumashima. Sometimes in my reflections on these events I wonder if our present day high school and college students are aware of the gift they have received from the Greatest Generation.

The 1944-45 school year at CCCA was drawing to a close, and the time arrived to begin celebrating the achievement of getting a high school diploma. The traditional senior class picnic was held in a coastal setting among wind blown scrub oaks near Rockport, about 30 miles north of Corpus Christi. It was an all day affair with a barbeque lunch and many outside games to test our wits and stamina. The faculty and many underclassmen were there to help us celebrate our last days in high school. We went home bone-tired, but happy.

It was also time to select the honor graduates of the senior class. There was no question about who would be Valedictorian. Johnny Golla was an exceptionally intelligent and hard-working student who racked up high grades as well as touchdowns. After military service, I believe he became an electrical engineer and a good family man. Unfortunately he died prematurely of a heart attack. As a physician, it grieves me to think about the chasm between our ability to recognize and treat occult coronary disease and extend lives now as opposed to then.

Father Albert Schreiber, our principal, then announced that the award of Salutatorian was so close between me and Walton McCarthy that the faculty had a difficult time coming to a decision. I suspect that the grade point average between us had to be carried out 3 or 4 decimal places. I truly wish he had been selected instead of me because my salutatory address was a disaster. Halfway through my text, I became faint and my vision faded, and I heard myself say, "I'm sorry but I can't go on." My pride was hurt. I felt sorry for my parents, my sister, my teachers and everyone in the audience. I wouldn't have to waste time in medical school studying the subject of panic attacks, but if they needed a lecturer I could address the subject very well! From that point on, I made a subconscious decision to fully understand any subject upon which I was asked to speak.

As if that disaster was not enough, I entered the next life challenge that would lower my self-esteem even further. The war in the Pacific was still raging because the Japanese Empire was prepared to fight to the bitter end. Victory would require an invasion of their homeland which would mean that thousands more American lives would be lost in that effort. When I graduated, I was still seventeen and would be for the next 8 months. I had enrolled in the Army Specialized Training Program, a program for high school graduates too young to be eligible for active duty. I presume it was designed to make the 17-year-olds more military ready and to provide a testing ground for selecting those who possessed special talents and leadership abilities. After a regular induction ceremony, physical exam and psychological testing, we were officially inducted into the Army, but not eligible for active duty.

My destination would be the ASTP corps at Texas A&M College where we lived in dormitories under regular military discipline. It was good preparation for what was to come. My first roommates were Cadet Abbot from Welch, Louisiana, and later Cadet Maley from Manor, Texas. I thrived on the military and physical education aspects of the program but academically I was lost. I found myself in an engineering curriculum without any advanced high school math, physics or chemistry. I lasted ninety days before my calculus grades fell short of the minimum requirement. I was sent home to await my call to active duty when I reached my eighteenth birthday. My self-esteem was at an all-time low.

On August 15, 1945, shortly after the atomic bombs were dropped on Hiroshima and Nagasaki, the Japanese Empire surrendered to the Allied powers and World War II was officially over. There was tumultuous joy in the cities and streets of America. At great cost in suffering and human life, our freedom was once again preserved.

My return home from A&M was less painful than I thought it would be due to everyone's preoccupation with the season's fifth hurricane. The storm made landfall in Port O'Conner on August 28, 1945, with sustained winds of 110 mph. My parents had taken refuge in the Plaza Hotel across Leopard Street from my dad's store. I joined them there and was watching Leopard Street through the front door of the hotel when a young Navy Wave came out of the Nixon Café and attempted to cross Leopard Street to our hotel. Leopard Street was like a wind tunnel between the two tall buildings, and the young woman was blown off her feet and swept some 20 yards down the street. A young Naval officer standing in our group ran out and rescued her and was able to get her back to our lobby by working his way, hanging on from one parking meter to the next, until they were safely inside.

The Army soon informed me that I would not be called to active duty and basic training until I reached age 18. I did not want to endure a six-month gap in my education. I called on our family friend, Dr. George McCulley, now registrar at Texas A & I College in Kingsville, to help me with a late application and begin a pre-med major in the Fall of 1945. My Dad drove me to Kingsville and helped me unload my bags at the dorm. In my assigned dormitory suite, we met a fellow freshman from Alice, Texas, who would have a major impact on Sarah's and my life in the distant future. His name was C. C. (Charlie) Winn and I will relate what the future held for both of us as time goes by. John Moothart from Harlingen, Paul Ryan and Eugene Mixon from Pawnee, were our roommates. John passed away from cancer a few years ago and I've lost track of Ryan and Mixon, but Charlie and I, and our families, have spent lots of time together in the last 20 years and what wonderful years they have been!

I started a pre-med curriculum at A & I determined to work hard and follow in my Uncle David's footsteps. I loved the friendly, non-threatening atmosphere of the college, which had only about 1400 students in the entire school. The natural gas engineering program, one of only two good programs in the country, was outstanding. The science department was very good and I really enjoyed Biology, taught by Dr. Bogusch, who was also the Pre-Med advisor and took a real interest in his pre-medical students. Life was good and became even more so after I often began to notice a really lovely brunette co-ed in the cafeteria line at lunchtime. I found out her name was Jo Ann Irwin from Floresville, and I was smitten. I was fortunate enough to finally meet her and actually take her to a local hangout, T-Jacs, for a soda and one movie date before the semester was over. Wayne Cole (BMOC - Big Man On Campus) and John Moothart, both Harlingenites, also dated Jo Ann. Wayne was a great trumpet player and led a dance band called The Lamplighters. They played for most of our campus dances. After we moved to the Rio Grande Valley, I would get to know Wayne again as an independent insurance agent. His son, Rick, dated my daughter, Catherine, in high school, and much later married her, but Wayne unfortunately didn't live to see that. Another of Wayne's escapades involved flying his plane under the Arroyo Colorado bridge at Rio Hondo. Wayne did not indulge in dull moments.

I was unable to begin the Spring semester at A & I because of my call to active duty in the Army. I was inducted in San Antonio and traveled by troop train to Camp Lee, Virginia, for 18 weeks of rigorous physical and military training with regular hours, exercise, sleep, and Army food. My 158 high school pounds turned into 189 pounds of hard muscle, and I morphed into a new model.

I was wishing that Jo Ann could see me then. We corresponded a few times as friends and I looked forward to seeing her again some day. I think she had a high school sweetheart who was serving in the Navy, although she never talked about him.

I haven't mentioned that I had learned to play the clarinet and was a band member at CCCA, when football and basketball didn't occupy my time. I also played in the A&I band the one semester I was there. I was never a 1st chair player, but I was good enough for 2nd or 3rd chair and to bring out the harmony. I was really tone deaf and couldn't carry a tune in a basket! Alas, some can and some can't, but I did enjoy music. The Army and the country were celebrating a new era of peace after 4 years of war and strife... Bandsmen were needed to furnish the music, so I volunteered to enter military band training and enjoy my clarinet instead of a rifle. It was a great choice, and I was having a wonderful time playing *Stars & Stripes*, the *Colonel Bogey March* and the *Star Spangled Banner*. My best friend at that time was fellow bandsman John Wilson from Chickasha, Oklahoma. Our friendship clicked, and we had a great time going to the USO and dancing with local girls and making an occasional trip to the city of Richmond. John eventually became a dentist and I lost track of him.

Then another major event occurred in my life. The Army issued an order to demobilize the Reserve Corps. I was a reservist on active duty. I had to suddenly make a choice to enlist for a minimum of 2 years in the regular Army or be a deactivated reservist who would still have a two-year military service obligation in the future. It took me about two minutes to know I wanted to get on with pre-med, get near home and my family, and possibly see Jo Ann again. The Fall semester had already started at A&I, but the fortuitous relationship that began with Dr. McCulley, in Austin, when I was a toddler, saved me once again and I was accepted for late admission into the Fall semester of 1947 to continue my pre-med studies. I had made the right choice and would later fulfill my two year military obligation as an Air Force surgeon in the Philippines.

When I arrived in Corpus Christi after my discharge, I didn't waste any time getting back to A&I, as the semester had already started. Many veterans of the war were returning to school and dormitory space was critical. I was assigned to a barracks at the Kingsville Naval Air Station. My roommate was Claude Guinn from a farming family in Edcouch, Texas. Claude turned out to be a fine fellow, and I enjoyed his company. Life at the remote dorm wasn't nearly as much fun as being on the campus in the thick of things. We had to ride a bus to class and missed the camaraderie of the main campus. I seldom saw Charlie Winn and my former roommates as we all had different majors. I did get to see Jo Ann more often, and we had an occasional date, but I didn't feel she was really interested in me.

About this time I met Orin Kutner Westbrook, another pre-med student who was a somewhat older and wiser World War II veteran. He was a Marine veteran who had just resumed civilian life. He was concerned about the impact of so many returning veterans potentially applying for admission to medical school. He felt transferring to a university that included a School of Medicine would be an advantage as we would not be strangers to their admissions committee. We started an application process to such schools, and Kutner was accepted at Baylor, and I was accepted at Tulane in New Orleans for the Fall semester of 1947. When I later found out there were 7000 applications for 129 places in my Class of 1953, I felt Kutner was prophetic beyond his years, and I've been forever grateful to him. He ultimately practiced Obstetrics and Gynecology in Houston, and I spoke once with him but never stayed in close contact.

During the Spring semester of 1947, school was going well, I was motivated by my acceptance at Tulane, and Jo Ann seemed a little more interested in me. I couldn't believe it when she asked me to be her escort for the Lantana Ball. The Lantana Court was composed of a Queen and four Lantana Ladies who were elected from the student body. My self-esteem had risen to an all-time high! My parents allowed me to have the family car for that weekend. Jo Ann's family, including her older sister, Frances Irwin Pederson, a former A&I student from Los Fresnos, Texas were all in attendance. The Ball was a great success and my confidence zoomed as Jo Ann's escort. The semester ended soon, and we returned to our family homes for the Summer vacation.

Big changes were about to occur in my life. A letter arrived from Tulane University of Louisiana accepting me into the College of Arts & Sciences to pursue a pre-medical curriculum for the Fall Semester of 1947. I was ecstatic! I would be attending a prestigious university with an outstanding medical school. I would be far from home in pursuit of a career that I was certain would be right for me. I could see myself as I saw my Uncle David, empowered with the knowledge to make a difference in people's lives. This opportunity served as an entry into the most intimate relationships that people have with their families, their careers and with each other based on trust and the Hippocratic Oath. I felt so blessed. I prayed for the strength to accomplish the task before me. I was a very happy young man.

As the Summer drew to a close, I concentrated on getting ready to leave for my first year of pre-med at Tulane. I was to travel by train, and it was a trip I would never forget. We were traveling through the farmlands of southern Louisiana when I felt a terrible heat on the train window. The train began to slow down rather abruptly in this rural area and soon came to a stop. Many of us detrained to find a horrific scene of death and destruction. Two related families in separate vehicles were traveling tandem to a picnic when the driver of the lead car decided he could beat the train to a crossing. Tragically, he was dead wrong. The train hit the rear end of the car causing the gas tank to explode. The car was instantly a big ball of flame trapping all of the occupants inside. I shall never forget the sight of those upright bodies, still in their seats, engulfed in flames. Neither shall I forget the weeping and wailing of the other family members as they arrived to witness the horrible demise of their kin.

I would not be alone in the big city of New Orleans, as my mother's first cousin, Mary Hawn Perdue, daughter of Uncle Jim and Aunt Jo Hawn, had lived there for many years with her husband Gordon Perdue and their daughter, Mary Gordon. They would be my family a long way from home, and they treated me like family from the moment I arrived. They had already found a room for me on the corner of Freret and Pine, just a block off of Broadway, and four blocks from the main campus. Tulane's student dormitories were reserved for women and those students on athletic scholarships. One of the joys of living in the University neighborhood was the various convenient boarding houses run by neighborhood women who cooked scrumptious Louisiana-style meals. Dinner was always on time and began with a traditional bowl of soup. Lively conversation brought on by students from various origins and different locales, in pursuit of a variety of academic goals, was an education in itself. I was a very happy fellow.

This new room included a roommate whom I had never met but with whom I would form a fast friendship. His name was Earl Hargroder, Jr., and he was from the heart of Cajun country, Church Point, Louisiana. Earl was a Pharmacy major at Loyola University. Loyola was next door to Tulane, and the two schools shared a common property line facing St. Charles Avenue. It was not unusual to have a roommate from a different university.

The setting for both schools was truly beautiful with the gigantic shade trees on campus, looking out toward Audubon Park, with picturesque trolleys chugging along St. Charles with their harsh bells clanging at every intersection. I always want to take a trolley ride when returning for reunions to remind me of my school days there and the many times I rode the trolley to the downtown school.

I really wasn't interested in the fraternity scene. I always felt hurt for those who, for one reason or another, failed to be invited into the pledge class. Nevertheless, I went to a Beta Theta Pi rush party apparently due to Vincent Tarlton, my old friend from Corpus, being an active brother in that group. Phi Kappa Sigma invited me to a rush party, and I met some fellows with whom I enjoyed conversing. One of them was Grover Lafayette Bynum, Jr., from Henryetta, Oklahoma. Grover was a fellow rushee who was also in pre-med. Our friendship would endure these sixty-seven years through our phone chats, one as recent as this morning.

Grover's father's roots were in Georgia, where he was an attorney when a decision was made to go West and settle the family in Oklahoma. Grover's mom was widowed at an early age when her husband died of peritonitis in the pre-antibiotic era. Grover had four sisters, three older and one younger, and he became the father-figure in that fine family. He always treated them with great love and respected their opinions in all family matters. Helene and Patricia have passed on, but Natalie and Eleanor still stay in close touch with their brother.

Grover was well known in the football world. As a high school quarterback, he led the Henryetta Hens to the Oklahoma State championship. Coach Henry Frnka of Tulsa University took notice. Later, when Frnka went to Tulane as Head Coach, Grover would play an important role, living in the athletic dorm, scouting, tutoring and general morale-building for the team.

After his high school graduation in 1945, Grover joined the Navy and ultimately played football at Great Lakes Naval Base. A

34

knee injury there ended his playing career, and he opted for college, as I had done, to begin his pre-med studies. I visited him at the dorm often and became somewhat familiar with college athletics from the inside. We had some pre-med classes together and saw each other at Phi Kap functions, and our friendship grew slowly, but surely. During exam time, we would often study late into the night and end up drinking coffee and eating pie at the Toddle House around 2 a.m. We still love to stay up late and talk about old times when we visit one another. Our wives are great friends and that pleases us and makes for extra good times when we get together.

During the latter part of the Spring semester in 1948, my roommate Earl moved closer to Loyola, and I got a new roommate, Eddie van Amerongen. Eddie was an architectural student who was related to Earl's uncle, a monsignor in Rayne, Louisiana. Eddie had lived through the German occupation of the Netherlands and had some traumatic experiences at that time. I had recruited him for the Phi Kap pledge class the following year. I wanted him to be a part of the American campus scene. Unfortunately, the initiation ceremonies brought memories of the German occupation and Eddie left the fraternity. I also wanted to leave, because I felt responsible for his "déjà vu' experience. Earl Hargroder told me Eddie had gone on to make a fine architect, and I heard from him once, but have lost track of him since.

The Summer of 1948 found me headed back to Corpus Christi, to help Dad at the store and to enjoy a mid-Summer break with my mom at Uncle David's cabin at Hunt, Texas. The cabin was on property that belonged to the Lang family from Kerrville. Mrs. Lang was a widow with two sons, Garland and Bobby. My Uncle David had met the Lang's when he was in pre-med at Schreiner Institute, and they became good friends. Many years later they had allowed him to build a small cabin near their family home, and I often went there with Gama, my mother and sister Jeanne. The cabin was just high enough above the river to avoid the floods that inevitably followed heavy rains in the Hill Country. The Guadalupe River was spring fed from a north and south fork that came together in front of the Lang Lodge and Uncle David's cabin. The north fork was cool and the south fork was warmer. One could sit at the fork and choose cool water or warm water depending on the moment's desire, or choose to swim down stream for an intermediate temperature.

Jo Ann was very much on my mind after a year at Tulane, and Mom agreed to chaperone a trip to the cabin if Jo Ann would agree to go. We spent a wonderful weekend and got to know each other better, but nothing serious developed. I saw her again later that Summer in San Antonio, when I came over from Kerrville to meet Harry Stuth and his girl friend, Joyce, whom he later married. We planned to double date that night. The only problem was an ingrown toenail that was really bothering me. I remembered that Ralph Cameron, Tulane Medical Class of 1950, was interning at the Robert B. Green Hospital in San Antonio. He was an older Nu Sigma Nu medical fraternity brother from Tulane. I told Harry that Ralph could probably fix my toe so that we could go dancing that night with Jo Ann and Joyce. We checked into the ER at the Green and asked for Dr. Cameron, who shortly appeared on the scene and was delighted to know he had a subject for his first toenail operation. I signed the operation permit considering it was only my toe, thinking nothing too bad could go wrong. To his credit, Dr. Cameron completed the operation, interrupted only by short absences to leave the scene for a few moments to review his surgical textbook. He didn't have too much to say about post-operative care, such as "stay off the foot for the next 24 hours and keep it elevated on a pillow", so Harry and I took our dates to an outdoor dancing garden and danced the night away. I wasn't a very happy camper the next morning with one foot twice as big as the other and throbbing with pain. I wasn't even in medical school yet and already had my first lesson in post-op care. But we had a grand time!

Summer was drawing to a close, and I was busy getting ready for my second year at Tulane. My folks bought a brand new 1947 Ford Sedan for me to take to school. I found out I could make it to New Orleans in 14 hours, even though there were no freeways and most of the highways were only one lane in each direction. Many times I would get on the Bolivar Ferry at Galveston and take a drive that hugs the coast highway to Port Arthur, traveling over the highest bridge in Texas at Bridge City. I occasionally reversed direction and traveled north on that same route. The drive was a real study of a primitive Texas coastline, featuring sandy beaches, all varieties of coastal birds, boats and habitations. Sadly that road, State Highway 87, was washed away by Hurricane Ike and has never been repaired. One can still cross Galveston Bay on the Port Bolivar Ferry to Highway 87, but one has to turn north at High Island and take State Highway 124 to Stowell and Winnie, which rejoins State Highway 73 to Port Arthur. Then one can again experience the high bridge on into Orange and cross the Sabine into Louisiana on I-10; a cumbersome route, but delightful when one has the time to enjoy traveling.

My second year at Tulane would find me living in the Phi Kap fraternity house at 700 Broadway. My new roommate was Bill Jameson from Camden, Arkansas. His older brother Jack also had lived in the fraternity house and had started medical school one year ahead of us. Grover and I would keep an eye on Jack's progress as we were following in his footsteps. We applied to med school to enter as freshmen in the Fall of 1949, and fortunately we were both accepted for the class of 1953.

At about that time, we began to see more of another pre-med student from Camden, Arkansas, James K. "Buddy" Patrick. Bud, as I liked to call him, was president of his Sigma Alpha Epsilon fraternity chapter and also a future medical school classmate in the class of 1953. The three of us began to see more of each other forming friendships that would last a lifetime. Bud and I would become roommates through the first two years of medical school, first as freshmen at Mrs. Tait's house on Zimple Street, and as sophomores in the Nu Sigma Nu Medical Fraternity house on St. Charles Avenue.

I have to mention Dr. Karlem Reiss, Professor of Physics at Tulane. Dr. Reiss' physics classes and exams were tough, but he was a great teacher. He was also a great Phi Kap alumnus, and he was our fraternity faculty sponsor. He spent quite a bit of time at our fraternity house keeping an eye on behavior problems and counseling us about keeping on the right track toward our goals of becoming educated and mature adults. Dr. Reiss, also known as "Ducky", because of his slew-footed walk, was a bachelor so he could afford the time he gave us and we certainly benefited from his efforts. Remember that I had never had a course in physics in my life so I was particularly grateful for his guidance. He was to remain active on the faculty and in the fraternity for many years after we left Tulane and was duly honored for his contributions to a wholesome student life.

Tulane had a great football team in the Fall of 1948. I was playing in the band and standing near the goalpost waiting to march at halftime during the Alabama game. I witnessed Tulane score three touchdowns against the Crimson Tide within two minutes. Tulane scored a touchdown and kicked the extra point. Alabama fumbled the kickoff, Tulane recovered and passed for a touchdown on the next play. After the next kickoff, Alabama's first down pass was intercepted and run back for a 3rd touchdown, followed by another extra point. Score Tulane 21-Alabama 0. The second half was less exciting, but Tulane won handily. We also played Notre Dame, coached by Frank Leahy, but lost a close one 12-6. We beat our archrival, Louisiana State University, 47-0. It was a great year on the gridiron for the Green Wave.

Going home for Christmas was always an exciting time. Acceptance in medical school seemed to portend the kind of life I so admired in my Uncle David. His life changed drastically when he informed my family that he was about to marry Mabel Hall, a widow with two grown children and a set of twins age 12. The oldest boy was Pat, about 21 at the time, and a daughter we all called Little Mabel who was a senior in high school. The twin boys were Bill and Ike. Uncle David adopted the twins. The bride's brother was a Methodist minister in Mathis, Texas, where we all met for the grand occasion and a chance to meet our new relatives. I thought Little Mabel was the prettiest girl I'd ever seen, and I was proud to claim her as a cousin. Pat came to Corpus Christi later on and worked with my dad for a while. Unfortunately, he was quite ill with malignant hypertension and died from a stroke a short time later. I didn't keep up with Little Mabel's academic life, but she eventually married Frank McMillan, a very successful oilman and settled in Corpus Christi. The twin boys went back to San Marcos, with Aunt Mabel and Uncle David and finished high school there. Ike became an attorney and settled in Dallas, but seemed more interested in refurbishing old apartments and houses and was very successful. He married a lovely girl from Venezuela, who became Irma White, and they lived happily for many years until Ike suffered a serious stroke and passed away shortly thereafter. Sarah and I visited them many times and remembered them as a very happy couple. They never had any children. We visited Irma a few times after Ike's death but have not been back to Dallas in many years.

Bill, Ike's twin was much harder to keep up with, although we get a Christmas card from him and his wife Susan every year. He went to medical school and finished a program at Columbia University in surgery of the brain and nervous system in New York City. Although fully trained in one of the top centers of the medical world in a very difficult specialty, I think his dad was greatly disappointed when he chose to settle in El Paso. On a much smaller scale, I'm sure my dad felt the same when I chose to go to Rio Hondo, after he had invested a great deal in my education. The hearts of young men who want to make a difference in the world see it differently than the older ones who have made peace with circumstances as they exist. It does take an exceptional person to make those kinds of dreams work, but I have seen it happen and because of such young men and women it will continue to happen. I am sure he was ultimately proud of me and my career of helping people in the Rio Grande Valley.

This is a goodtime to write about my father, John A. Ferris, Sr., the fourth child and son of Saadi and Sophia Ferris. He was born in Austin, September 14, 1900. At the age of five, he and two of his older brothers were sent to Lebanon to live with relatives and learn the family culture and the Arabic language. He remained there for four years and when he came home to Austin, he was fluent in Arabic. He never spoke Arabic at home, but if I accompanied him to gatherings of his family, he spoke fluently to his relatives and his Lebanese friends. Dad and I occasionally visited a produce market further out on Leopard Street, run by the Sam Ferris family. They were not relatives of ours but had the same last name. I heard him speak Arabic with the folks out there on several occasions. I never heard a word of Arabic in our home unless he was talking on the phone to one of our relatives. As I look back, I have a deep regret that I was not allowed to learn about this Middle Eastern culture. I suspect it was based on deep-rooted prejudices related to the mixed marriage of western and Middle Eastern cultures. My dad always ingrained in my thinking that the Lebanese were descendants of the Phoenicians, who were the world's first traders and gave us the first alphabet and the written word. He spoke with great pride about these profound contributions to mankind.

My dad was very gregarious with his customers and with the business community in Corpus Christi. He was very active in civic work. He was President of the Corpus Christi Rotary Club; a member of Salvation Army Board; received the Silver Beaver Award for his work in scouting; and ultimately a major player in the reformation of Corpus Christi's government from a

40

commission-managed city to a city manager form of government. Up to that time George Parr, of San Diego in Duval County, had a significant influence on the policies established by the Mayor and Commissioners. Many of our leading citizens did not feel these policies were conducive for the growth of Corpus Christi. A recall election was held and a new city government was put in place. Robert T. Wilson was the new Mayor and the new commissioners were Wesley Seale, Raymond Henry, Captain Joe Dawson and my dad, John A. Ferris, Sr. This episode in Corpus Christi history was no small feat. The candidates received many death threats and threats that their children would be kidnapped. The candidates were not about to be deterred. Dawson was the World War II hero of the Battle of Dawson's Ridge in the European theater. George Parr had met his match. Corpus Christi is now a thriving city of almost 300,000 people and an important shipping port for the oil production of the Eagle Ford discovery in South Texas.

Wilson was head of the La Gloria Corporation. His brother was President of General Motors. Wesley Seale and Raymond Henry were solid Corpus Christians and my Dad was a beacon for doing the right thing. That was the beginning of a City Manager form of government in Corpus Christi.

The Summer vacation was passing quickly. It was about that time when I learned about Mary Gwen Foran. My memory is somewhat cloudy about the circumstances, but I believe I first knew of her when she attended Camp Arrowhead, and I was working nearby at Camp La Junta. My sister Jeanne knew her at Incarnate Word Academy and told me that she was a very fine girl. When we were both back in Corpus Christi, I was able to get a date with her and then began to see and date her more often.

When it was time to return to Tulane, I was hopelessly in love with her and took her picture back to school and wrote her often. Her family entrusted me to take her and her younger brother Bill on a road trip to East Texas to make preparations for a family gathering with her parents and her Uncle Bill at their cabin in East Texas. They were a convivial family and the brothers, Ding and her Uncle Bill, loved to sing and harmonize. Her mother Marge was a lively outgoing woman who enjoyed life and was very sharp. We had a grand time swimming in a nearby lake, cooking outdoors, singing and telling lots of stories. I truly loved her and her family.

The Summer ended, and after she graduated as Valedictorian of her class, she went off to Stanford, and I went to my first year of medical school at Tulane. We dated often during the Christmas holidays of that year and everything seemed fine. She was excited about Stanford and her experiences in California, and I felt the same about my first year in medical school.

When the Spring semester was over, and I came home for the Summer something was different. I did not get to see her until late the evening of my first day home because of some errands my mother had asked me to do. When I finally arrived at her home, she did not feel like coming down stairs to see me. I was devastated. I did not know if she was upset because I put my mother's chores before seeing her or if her feelings about me had changed? I suspected the latter. The next day we visited on the front steps of her home, and she explained to this dumb old boy the difference between loving someone and being "in love" with someone. I never even thought about that. I think young guys have feelings beyond their understanding. With this new understanding of affairs of the heart, I knew that I was "in love" with her and that she "loved me"; a recipe for eventual disaster or life long torment. I had experienced my third great hurt; the first two being the salutatory address and the ASTP disaster. Somehow I recovered slowly by working at Camp La Junta for the rest of the Summer .

Jim McCutchon recently informed me that Mary Gwen is the happily married mother of six children. Together with her husband, Gerald Brummit, Mary Gwen endowed her alma mater, Incarnate Word Academy, where she was valedictorian, with a generous gift. I believe they reside in or near Coronado, California, where she has been very active in community affairs.

When we started our first year in medical school, Buddy Patrick and I had arranged to room together at Mrs. Tait's house on Zimple Street, which bordered the Sophie Newcomb Campus in the university neighborhood. It was just a few blocks from the Richardson Memorial Building where Tulane Medical School held freshman and sophomore classes. Ira Campbell from Coushatta, Louisiana, lived across the hall from us. Ira provided us with small town Louisiana humor in his role as the country doctor-to-be. He was a classic example of the country doctor, down to the gold pocket watch and chain, which he wore secured in his vest. When most of us looked for fun on Saturday nights, Ira had on his pajamas by 8 p.m. and was in bed listening to the Grand Ole Opry. He was refreshingly pure country. He still makes our class reunions with his lovely wife Reva.

Jerry Fortenberry and Bob Culpepper, both from Mississippi, lived next door and shared a bathroom with us. All-in-all we had a very compatible upstairs group at the Tait House.

Our first day of medical school was pulsating with anticipation. After an orientation address by anatomy professor Dr. Harold Cummins the doors of the anatomy lab swung open and our nostrils were filled with the odor of formaldehyde. We would live and breathe that smell for the next four months until we had uncovered the name and location of every organ, muscle, nerve and blood vessel in the body. We were allowed to make up our own table teams, enabling Grover, Buddy and I to stick together. We were fortunate in finding an enjoyable newlywed from Mississippi, Laverne Alexander, whose sense of humor enabled him to put up with our chiding concerning his matrimonial state. We four were a solid team of friendship and mutual support. We named our Cadaver "Ol' Good Buddy" and wondered what sort of life he led. We did have great respect for what his life may have been like and even more respect for his contribution to our education. So much so that Sarah and I have donated our mortal bodies to a medical school.

Before I go any further into that first year, I have to introduce one more significant student who would be a lifelong friend to our triumvirate. He was from Nashville, Arkansas, and his name was Reginald C. Ramsay, better know as Rex. He was a star fullback in high school but early on decided that becoming a good doctor was the most important thing in the world to him. He threw himself into the study of medicine the same way he threw himself into the opposing line in football. I was intimidated when I first called on him because he had already read several chapters in one of our first textbooks. Nevertheless, that first encounter with Rex convinced me that I wanted to be his friend. I loved Arkansas because of all my family connections there and also because the Ozarks were so beautiful and home to my dear mother.

Later in that year a surprise phone call came from one of the De Pineda debutantes, Caroline Tompkins, from Corpus Christi. She was to be presented at the annual De Pineda Ball and wondered if I would be her escort. It took me about one second to accept. Deep in my heart I felt a wave of warm healing begin to ease the pain of the previous Summer. Caroline was the angel of mercy who helped me through a difficult time. She and Mary Gwen were presented as debutantes at the same Buccaneer Ball. During the first dance after the presentation, Mary Gwen and I made eye contact for a moment, and she gave me a parting gift I shall always remember, but won't recount here. Those were wonderful but difficult times.

Grover, Buddy and I were recruited by the Phi Chi medical fraternity as well as by Nu Sigma Nu, and we spent some serious contemplative hours trying to make a decision. Jack Schneider, a sophomore from Austin, Texas, was the Nu Sig rush chairman.

His dad and my dad were boyhood friends in Austin, so I felt a connection. I think Grover and Bud also felt more comfortable with the Nu Sig program. Dr. Alton Ochsner, the world famous dynamic professor of surgery at Tulane, was also a Nu Sig, and I believe the stories of him spending some time with the brothers at the fraternity house also influenced our decision to pledge Nu Sigma Nu and share time with such a renowned teacher. Bud, Grover and I chose to pledge Nu Sigma Nu. Rex pledged Phi Chi and was to be fraternity brothers with some outstanding classmates such as Ken Moss and Pete Phillips from Lake Charles, Billy Hayden from Shreveport, and Clyde Smith from Alabama.

Our Class of 1953 is unique in Tulane Medical School history for its record of sticking together with annual reunions after our Fiftieth in 2003. This record is largely due to the efforts of Pete Phillips and Ken Moss who worked tirelessly with their wives, Ann and Wanda, to stay in touch with everyone and organize an enjoyable venue for our get-togethers. Our 2012 reunion was held at the Gulf Hills resort in Ocean Springs, Mississippi. Nineteen of us were there and we had a marvelous time. Bob "Crazy" Carter and his friend Judy Howell hosted the affair. They arranged superb restaurants and shopping tours in this quaint resort town. John Jackson filled us in on his talent and secrets about making and playing real gourd banjos. Mostly our joy is in visiting with each other, recounting old stories and jokes, vignettes of school and finding out how we currently spend our time. Our life partners probably think we're a bit nuts but they do tolerate our enjoyment of these reunions. Tulane always sends an alumni representative to stay in touch with our lives, and we appreciate the Mother House caring about how we're doing. Tulane's logo is a Mother Pelican on her nest nurturing and protecting three chicks. Underneath this scene is the Latin inscription "Non Sibi Sed Suis" which translates – "not for herself alone but for her own!" We do feel she cares, and we do care for those who follow in our footsteps.

I want to pause here for a little levity. Ken Moss and Pete Phillips were lifelong friends having come up through the Lake Charles school system, playing high school football together, college years and certainly as medical school classmates, residencies at Charity Hospital, even to the point of serving together in Korea as Battalion surgeons. Ken passed away two years ago but before that, Pete loved to tell this story about his dear friend. "A very wealthy traveler was passing through the city of Lake Charles when he was unfortunately overcome with an acute gallbladder attack. He proceeded to the emergency room of a nearby hospital where he was informed that emergency surgery was indicated in order to avoid gallbladder rupture. Realizing this was a critical moment, the wealthy gentleman let it be known that he was able to pay for the very best surgeon available. When the unfortunate patient inquired as to whom that might be the prompt answer to his query was 'Dr. Ken Moss - - - - - - - - - when he's sober!' Whereupon the somewhat shocked victim of the gall bladder attack asked, 'who might be the next best surgeon in Lake Charles to solve his dilemma?' 'Ken Moss when he's drunk!' came the quick reply." Of course, the reader knows that is NOT a true story, but good for a heart warming laugh! Ken and Wanda have three sons who are now surgeons in Lake Charles, carrying on a family tradition. What a contribution this family has made to their community. Pete Phillips, though retired, still serves as a volunteer in the Shriner's Crippled Children's Clinic. His beautiful wife, Ann, has suffered lovingly through countless reunions and been a great contributor to our class spirit along with Wanda Moss who showed great courage and love when she attended our 2011th reunion banquet after Ken's death.

Pete is still the engine that keeps our group together. Tulane Medical Alumni Association will host our 60th reunion. Who knows what will happen after that. I'm getting vibes that we should possibly shut it down after the 60th before it morphs into a mourning meeting. I think we'll know what to do when the time comes rather than write it off now. Until then, we have many wonderful memories and classmates.

Our second year as sophomores was still in the Richardson Building on the uptown campus. Biochemistry and pharmacology were big and challenging subjects during the Fall semester. If it hadn't been for Grover Bynum's morale building and study support, I might not have made it through that Fall. I gave up band participation in my freshman year to have more time for study, and I needed every minute of it. My poor preparation in high school was showing and I was struggling. I often found myself in prayerful moments asking Our Blessed Mother for help with the learning task before me. In my freshman year, I often attended daily Mass and Communion to gain our Lord's help that I might learn the necessary requisites to be a really fine physician.

I find myself in that mode even to this day. I am brought to the memory of the finest lecture that I can remember from medical school. The lecture was delivered by Dr. George Burch, a homegrown Louisiana boy who became a world-renowned Cardiologist by hard work and a gifted mind. He wrote a fine Primer of Cardiology that grounded us well in the basics of understanding heart disease. However, on this day he wandered into the subject of proper behavior of a physician burdened with the responsibility of life and death decisions for patients and their loved ones. He emphasized the awesome responsibility we bore and the gift of faith we received when patients and their loved ones actually bared their souls and placed their own and their families' lives in our hands to do the right thing! He drove that lesson home so well that I think about him every time I am facing that situation. As an older physician, I face it even more often because my patients are older, and I'm often talking to three generations of one family.

In fact, as I write this today, Easter Sunday, 2013, I took note of two of my patients in the obituary column of the local Sunday paper. One of them was the second person I met when I first considered practicing in the Rio Grande Valley fifty-five years ago. Then, as a young attorney, Martin Ferrero advised me that I would do well, and he counseled me for the rest of my career until he retired from the practice of law. I worked with his family through the last few years of his invalidism and helped them as we all agreed that his comfort and wishes to be spared some of modern medicine's tests and studies were not in his best interest. I marveled at the devotion of his housekeeper of 46 years, Rosa Mireles, who so wanted him to recover but also understood how his comfort and wishes to be at home were paramount in the equation of end-of-life care. She was a heroine in her role as caregiver and made his last days the best they could be.

The unique gift of being a good caregiver to the disabled and dying is a gift I have often noted in my years of practice, and there is no question in my mind that it is a step toward sainthood for those so endowed. Thank God for each and every one of them.

Returning to my story, after the Christmas holidays of our sophomore year, we began our first clinical experiences. We wore short brown lab coats to identify us as one of the lowest forms of clinical life. With a stethoscope, an otoscope and a reflex hammer tucked in our pocket, and a Merck Manual to answer questions that dumbfounded us, we entered the world of Clinical Medicine. Uncle David sent me some of his older equipment, which saved me money and increased the bond between us.

Our first important course was Physical Diagnosis. One of the younger faculty members would shepherd a small group of us, and we would learn how to carefully examine every part of the human body in great detail. We would also learn how to take a good history of the current illness, and we learned that accuracy in diagnosis depended as much or more on the quality of the patient's history than it did on the physical examination. To be a good physician, one has to listen carefully to the patient and ask the right questions. An axiom follows: "Listen to the patient – the patient is telling you what's wrong with him or her".

I have great admiration for the specialist who tells me he wants to talk to the patient before he makes any other suggestions or schedules any definitive procedures. I know that consultant has his priorities in order. One of my friends sent me a cartoon book showing various scenes of sophomore medical students learning to examine different systems of the body. Most of the cartoons were pretty routine, except for the young male student about to do his first pelvic exam on a female. The student was depicted with beads of sweat popping out on his forehead and a trembling hand trying to hold on to a vaginal speculum, all the while maintaining a professional countenance.

We had wonderful teachers in Obstetrics and Gynecology in our junior and senior years. Conrad Collins was head of the department and his younger brother Jason was second in command. They taught us how to be very proficient in this field by having us attend the clinics giving young mothers their six-week postpartum checkups. At that point, the women's reproductive anatomy had been stretched by a seven-pound infant and had not yet regained its normal tone. It was easy to outline the ovaries and the uterus while making sure there were no postpartum problems.

We had no shortage of clinical cases and deliveries to witness due to the one thousand babies born at Charity Hospital in New Orleans. I had delivered fifty infants by the time I left OB training in my junior year. My experience at Charity Hospital served me well because my first eleven years in practice included pre-natal care and Obstetrics.

I was highly complimented and surprised when the administrator of our hospital asked if I would render pre- and post-natal care and deliver his daughter's first born, even though there were board certified OB doctors on the hospital staff. Why would such an offer be made? In my mind, it has to do with how much a physician displays an attitude of concern for the well being of the patient. Given that most physicians have equal competence in what they are trained to do, what then separates one from another? Some might call it "bedside manner" but that is a frivolous over-simplification. I believe it is a matter of trust. This physician is listening to the patient's story and is totally focused on what the patient is telling him to the exclusion of any distractions. This physician will integrate the patient's story with the physical examination and lab work necessary to deduce the best answer, and as a result, the patient has a chance to be well, or at least, experience relief. If the physician cannot understand and solve a particular problem, the physician is quick to seek the opinion of a consultant who can help.

We second semester sophomore students were also beginning to attend more clinical conferences regarding diagnosis and treatment of various patients and their disorders. These conferences whet our appetites for more knowledge because we began to identify with real life situations and were beginning to feel the twinges of being real doctors.

Before we knew it, Summer was upon us. I was able to get a counselor job at Camp La Junta in Hunt, Texas. The camp was just a few miles from Uncle David's cabin on the South Fork of the Guadalupe River. I shared a cabin with another counselor, Bert Coleman, from La Feria, Texas, whom I would again meet when I settled there to practice. We supervised the campers in swimming, horseback riding, tennis, and archery. We acted as surrogates for their parents - seeing to it that they brushed their teeth, minded their manners, were civil to one another, and attended Church on Sunday if their parents made that request. Being a medical student, I was asked to help Nurse Julia Laakso in the infirmary during sick call and attend other minor injuries. Mrs. Laakso worked with Dr. Duan Packard from Kerrville, who visited the camp when necessary for more serious problems.

His brother, Dr. John Packard, practiced Urology in Harlingen, and I would one day be his patient. When I later became Chief of Staff at Valley Baptist Hospital in 1976, Dr. Packard would give me some very sound advice about physician and hospital relationships. Dr. Packard now sees me as his primary physician, an honor because he is one of the finest men I have ever known. His mind is sharp as a tack at age 94 and he is certainly a joy in my life. He lost his wife, Doris, from cancer, many years ago. They had three children and one of their sons died, but his daughter and remaining son stay in close touch with him and visit frequently. Those of us who know Dr. Packard well are touched by the renewal of his friendship with an old girlfriend, Barbara Blake, from Washington State. She lost her husband several years ago, and they occasionally spend time here and there visiting one another. It's a beautiful thing to see their companionship lighten the sorrow of a lost spouse.

Awhile after Jim McCutchon lost his wife, my sister Jeanne, well-meaning friends tried to match him with the perfect date. In desperation, he told his friends if they really wanted to make him happy to arrange a date with his old friend Dixie Tanguis, who was also widowed and living in Baton Rouge. In earlier years, Dixie and her husband also lived in Corpus Christi and were in the same parish family guild as Jim and Jeanne. The couples knew each other quite well and a perfect second chance was about to occur. When Jim told me about Dixie, I was thrilled for both of them. The match was perfect, and they had several happy years together before Dixie was stricken with a degenerating Neurological disorder and died in a state of total paralysis. Jim remodeled their home for her special needs and stuck by her side until her last breath. They were hero and heroine to the last; he in total devotion and she in uncomplaining acceptance. I am so humbled by their love and example, and I pray that Sarah and I can face whatever challenges are in store for us. Sarah is already being put to the test with severe rheumatoid disease that has put her on a walker and caused her much suffering.

I had a chance to go to San Antonio in 1952 and see Jo Ann for what would be our last date, although I didn't know that at the time. She was as beautiful and as sweet as ever, but whatever it is that lets two people know the time is right for them to commit to spend the rest of their lives together, just wasn't there. I had two more years of medical school, no money except paltry Summer earnings and whatever subsistence my parents provided.

As we began our junior year, Rex and I had secured extern jobs at a Catholic orphanage called Hope Haven in Marrero, across the Mississippi river from the city of New Orleans. We traveled on a ferry morning and evening to get to and from school every day of the week, including Saturdays. We earned our keep in exchange for taking sick calls from the orphans in the evenings. We earned breakfast, supper and a room with a bed and a desk. Many students performed paramedical work on the side to help with the cost of staying in school. Grover and Buddy secured externships at Baptist Hospital on Napoleon Avenue to help their cause.

I will never forget one morning when Rex and I missed the ferry, and it happened to be the same morning that Dr. Ochsner was giving a lecture to the entire class, the type of lecture one does not miss. We approached the closed auditorium doors with stealth waiting for an opportune moment when Jason, the slide projectionist, would dim the lights for the next slide, to slip undetected into a nearby open seat. At least, that was the plan, but as we all know the best laid plans of mice and men occasionally don't work out. Rex was about half way to his intended seat, when "The Big O" suddenly stopped in the middle of his lecture and called for the lights, thereby exposing my friend's clandestine journey to the entire class who were considerably amused and about to hear a scathing lecture on punctuality. No one was more qualified to give that lecture than Dr. Ochsner himself. He was punctual to a fault, always with pencil and paper, and a medical journal tucked in his lab coat pocket. He retired at 1 a.m. and arose to begin his day at 5 a.m., a talented dynamo of energy whose discipline enabled him to be a great teacher and a great surgeon.

"So, Mr. Ramsay, where have you been that would cause such a disruption of this surgery lecture and inconvenience to me and your classmates, all of whom seemed to have been here on time?"

Lamely, Rex offered a credible but unacceptable excuse. "I missed the ferry."

"How often does the ferry run, Mr. Ramsay?"

"Every 30 minutes, Sir."

"Have you considered the possibility of catching an earlier ferry to assure your timely arrival to classes such as this which have the sole intent of making you into a real doctor?"

"Yes sir, and I won't be late again."

"Thank you, Mr. Ramsay."

Our classmates got the message and amidst the distraction of the moment, I was able to slip into an empty seat unnoticed, something over which I still feel pangs of guilt.

Alton Ochsner was a giant in the field of surgery. He traveled in the company of George Crile from the Cleveland Clinic, Owen Wangensteen from the University of Minnesota, Will Mayo of the Mayo Clinic, and Robert Zollinger of Ohio State. These men were academic pioneers in their field who insisted on training surgeons for four or more years and supported the American College of Surgeons and the American Board of Surgery so the public would know how to identify well trained and capable doctors in matters of surgical disease.

I actually worked side by side with a young Air Force surgeon who would become one of these giants, though I didn't fully recognize it at the time. I admired his work ethic and his courage in taking on surgical challenges after only one year of residency, but I never imagined the depth of his ability in that field. His name was Arthur E. Baue from St. Charles, Missouri. He arrived at Clark AFB in the Philippines a short time after I did with his wife, Rosemary. They were a lovely couple and friendly enough to baby-sit our children for a few days when we traveled to Japan. Unfortunately, we lost track of them when we both returned to the States, and it was only recently that I discovered the history of his outstanding career as a surgeon. After completing his residency, he remained in academics, eventually becoming Professor of Surgery at Yale. After two years there, he moved to his hometown area as Professor of Surgery at St. Louis University. During his academic surgical career, he published 650 scientific articles, authored six textbooks of surgery, one of which was the original description of the Syndrome of Multi-Organ Failure. He served as President of the American College of Surgeons, President of the American Board of Surgery, and many lesser societies too numerous to mention. Unfortunately both he and Rosemary passed away some two years ago, so we will never see them on this earth. I would love to meet his children one day and learn more about their family life.

This specialty certification has spread to all the various disciplines of medicine, Pediatrics, Obstetrics and Gynecology and most of the sub-specialties such as ENT, Ophthalmology, Neurology, Orthopedics, etc. The specialty of family medicine includes the basics of most of the above and is particularly suited to distribute primary care to more rural areas and average size towns or to families who prefer one doctor for the entire family. This broader service also requires three years of training to cover the basics of Pediatrics, OB/GYN, Internal Medicine and minor surgery. The Family Practice Residency Program at Valley Baptist Hospital in Harlingen, Texas has done just that under the extraordinary leadership of Dr. Bruce Leibert and the full time faculty of Drs. Darryl White, Seth Patterson, Claudia Vasquez, Nina Torkelson, Peter Lazzopina and psychologist Dr. Steven

Johnson. This thoroughly Christian-oriented training program has graduated some 90 doctors of family medicine who are now serving in the various roles of family practice from Harlingen throughout the United States and in the mission field the world over. I am so proud to be associated with them and often feel it is a gift of which I am not worthy.

As we moved ahead in our junior year, we were assigned to an Internal Medicine service to take care of hospitalized patients. We learned to do comprehensive history and physical exams. I was assigned to the teaching service of Dr. Roy Turner at the Touro Infirmary just off St. Charles Avenue and across the street from the old Ochsner Clinic. A vignette of medical history made Dr. Turner believe that I might be an exceptional student when he asked our group if anyone happened to know what Sir William Osler had to say about the diagnosis of syphilis. I had become interested in medical history and had read a great deal about Doctor Osler's life. I knew the answer. Dr Osler said, "Know syphilis in all of its manifestations and all else clinical shall be added unto you". I think Dr. Turner was surprised, and I believe he was pleased to know there was interest in medical history in our group. Many of us became members of the History of Medicine Society, a group that promoted knowledge of medical history. Knowing history well is certainly a deterrent to repeating errors of the past. History also reveals that major advances in medicine were made by physicians who were gifted and imaginative; men and women who had the ability to look beyond the accepted knowledge of their day.

I was disappointed that our residents of today were unable tell me the story of Dr. Simmelweiss and childbed fever. Puerperal sepsis, as it appears in the medical literature, took the lives of many new mothers three to five days after childbirth when attended by horse and buggy doctors who rushed from the stable to the bedside to deliver an infant without washing their hands. Dr. Simmelweiss insisted on the simple practice of washing one's hands before touching the mother or her baby and what followed was a dramatic drop in the incidence of childbed fever and more importantly a significant drop in maternal mortality.

Dr. Edward Jenner observed that English milkmaids who had acquired cowpox from milking infected cows were spared the wrath of smallpox. He found that inducing cowpox material into the skin of healthy subjects protected them from developing the dreaded and often fatal disease of smallpox. The reason for this was because the poxes were so similar in their biologic structure that the human immune system could not differentiate them. Today the world is free of smallpox epidemics, and therein, lies the story of the world's first immunization program.

Our clinical years were becoming interesting as we spent more time with live patients, learning how the knowledge we gained in the basic sciences actually enabled us to understand what was happening in the ill patient. We began to see how this insight allowed us to take logical steps to try to correct what we found wrong. We felt the elation associated with relief and cure and began to learn how to handle the frustration of failure to cure. In the latter case, an important lesson learned was to comfort always.

The Christmas holidays were always welcome, but less exciting this time as there was no romantic interest with whom to share the celebration. Jim McCutchon and my sister seemed to be growing closer, and I was very happy about that because he was a fine man. His Catholic faith was strong, and he came from a fine family with strong values. I was happy to head back to school and get on about the business of becoming a doctor.

One of the most challenging classes we faced as seniors was one required appearance in the Saturday morning "Bull Pen". We started attending Bull Pen sessions as juniors but didn't have to present a case until we were seniors. Just you, your previously unknown patient, Dr. Ochsner, and an amphitheater seating junior and senior medical students, interns, residents and associate faculty members. A student was allowed thirty minutes to interview and examine the patient never seen before and then present the case to Dr Ochsner and the entire group in the amphitheater. It was a highly pressurized moment and a lesson in humility if one wandered too far off the problem. Every class member at our reunions can remember the case they presented on that day. They also remember the wisdom of the "The Big 'O'" as he was kind enough to stop short of the humiliation of a student, but rather kindly lead him to the best answer possible and then discuss appropriate treatment. I believe it was an exercise in motivation to learn for most of us.

One Saturday, Rex and I were seated in the bullpen audience, and I kept looking at the back of one individual's head and left shoulder trying to identify him. He had on a long white medical gown, which meant he was either faculty or a resident. When he later turned his head to the left, I was amazed to see Gary Cooper dressed as a doctor. He was a surgical patient of Dr. Ochsner who had invited him to attend the Bull Pen. Rex and I saw them leave Charity Hospital together to walk to the Orleans Club on Canal Street, some 10 blocks away. We thought it would be interesting to follow them and see the percentage of passers-by on Canal Street who would recognize the famous actor. We noted that only about 25% actually took about 10 steps, then turned around to see if what they thought they saw was reality. As Americans living in a world where radical terrorist groups openly threaten to kill us and destroy our freedom, our officials and first responders have urged us to increase awareness of our surroundings and promptly report any suspicious situations that might suggest danger. We must vastly improve awareness and better the 25% record of the Canal Street pedestrians.

Rex and I left Hope Haven in Marrero and came back to the city as our junior year came to a close. Rex was able to get an externship at Baptist Hospital with Bud and Grover. He also met a nursing student there by the name of Tee Patrick and fell hopelessly in love with her. Mary and Gordon Perdue allowed me to move in with them for the short time left in the semester. Their daughter Mary Gordon was away at school, so I had a place to live to finish out the junior year.

Jack Schneider had earned his room and board during his last two years of medical school by working in the lab at the Eye, Ear, Nose, and Throat Hospital just two blocks from the medical school and Charity Hospital. His job was to get up early and draw blood from patients going to surgery that day. It also involved coming in on Sunday afternoons to do lab work on patients going to surgery on Monday morning. The living quarters were decent and the food was good. Being so close to school was a real plus. Jack took me to meet Alice Saillard, the lab manager, and suggested that I would be a good man for the job. She hired me to start in the Fall and that made my senior year easier being close to the school.

I was truly enjoying the last semester of my junior year as we were constantly in contact with patients in real life situations. There were more and more lectures in the sub-specialties which explored new territory in Urology, Pediatrics, Proctology, Orthopedics, ENT, but still a heavy emphasis on continuing studies in Internal Medicine with lots of reading to do.

It was about this time that I met Sister Hayden, a lovely, lithe blonde from Shreveport, and a sister to Billy Hayden, our medical school student president. We began to date for Saturday night parties at the Nu Sig house and seemed to enjoy each other's company. When she asked me to come to Shreveport and spend the weekend with her and her family, I felt she was serious and I was honored but somewhat unsure of myself. I did accept her invitation and loved being with her and meeting her family. I hoped our relationship would grow and looked forward to seeing her again in the Fall as I began my senior year.

Shortly after I was home I received a phone call from Sarah Jane Allen. I knew her by name and appearance only. She asked if I would be a date for one of her college roommates who was visiting in her home. The girl was Sally Tally from Roswell, New Mexico. Sarah was supposed to go with Starr Pope, but he was called out of town. I arranged for my old friend Harry Stuth to escort Sarah Jane in lieu of Starr's absence. We were going to attend a party at Guy Warren's home. The following weekend Harry James and his orchestra were in town to play at the 'O' Club at the Corpus Christi Navel Air Station. My dad gave me 4 tickets so I called Sarah Jane and invited her and Sally to go with Harry and me to listen and dance to the music of this famous band and its trumpet-playing leader. Only this time I suggested that Harry be Sally's date and I would be Sarah Jane's escort. Something about Sarah Jane made me want to know her better. She was attractively beautiful, didn't put on any airs, soft spoken and fun to be with. I already knew I would be calling her for dates after Sally left. We had a grand evening dining and dancing to the music of the greatest dance band in America.

We were going out more frequently and began to realize how much we enjoyed doing things together. There were picnic trips to the beach, swimming in the surf, ukulele strumming and singing our favorite songs in the moonlight. Life was good and I was unusually happy in the company of this beautiful young woman. I was frequently a guest for backyard Bar-B-Ques at her parents' home when her dad put on one of his specialty feasts featuring shrimp cooked over open coals. They lived in a very modest frame home in an older part of town at 1613 Sixth Street, about 3 blocks from Six Points. The home was built just before the Great Depression and when times were really tough her parents moved in with her grandparents at their home on Tancahua Street, at the current site of the La Retama Library. When economic conditions improved, they were able to return to their home on Sixth Street.

Frank C. Allen, Jr. and his younger brother Evan Allen managed the Allen Furniture store in Corpus Christi, and Frank C. Allen, Sr., took over when his two sons served in World War II. Sarah Jane told me of her travels and life in the military during her high school years when she lived in seven different towns. The family did manage to get back to Corpus Christi for her senior year and graduation from Corpus Christi High School in 1947.

As the Summer of 1952 was drawing to a close, Sarah Jane and I were spending much more time together and realizing how similar our values were. She had no plans for marriage and envisioned herself running an orphanage in Mexico. More importantly, she had developed a real interest in the Catholic faith and wanted to explore the possibility of leaving her strong Methodist heritage and joining the Church. One of her roommates at Stephens College was Catholic, and she had felt very comfortable attending Mass with her and felt an inner pull toward becoming a Catholic This made me very happy, and subconsciously I could visualize a life with a person so dear and so compatible.

One evening we decided to see a movie entitled *Room For One More*, the story of a "yours, mine and ours" marriage that featured a very happy mother and father who ended up with a dozen children. We could see ourselves in a similar situation. As we parked in front of her home to say good night, we looked at each other from a safe distance and a very warm glow filled my heart and I said, "Will you marry me?" She gave a positive nod and a sweet "yes" and the rest is history. She told her folks that night and I told my folks the next morning. We were two happy people.

Then we talked about when that wedding might take place. The ideal time would be at the end of my senior year, right after graduation from medical school. Jimmy and Jeanne were planning to be married at the same time. Sarah had already signed a contract to teach 4th grade at Fisher Elementary School in Corpus Christi. We both had school years that would keep us very busy and help time fly. We would see each other at Christmas, and Sarah would come to New Orleans once in the Spring. Life was good except for one thing – I had to break the news to Sister Hayden. I felt she really cared about me, and I know I cared a great deal about her, but not in the same way or with the same confidence that I felt in my love for Sarah Jane.

Sister had taken a room on St. Charles just about three blocks from the Tulane campus. The house was classic New Orleans with an open front porch, and she was standing at the far end smiling as I approached. My heart ached as I walked toward her, and it must have shown on my face because her expression seemed to lose its glow. Her intuition was beginning to sense something was amiss. I told her about Sarah and that it wouldn't be right for me to continue to see her.

Sister always seemed to me to be a quiet and introspective person, and she certainly was that day. I really don't know how she ultimately processed this news. I hope and pray she handled it well and found someone with whom to share her life. I have not had any news of her since then.

Her brother Billy Hayden graduated near the top of our class and went on to a surgery residency at Scott and White Clinic in Temple, Texas. He married Elizabeth Domingue, a lovely girl from South Louisiana. They raised their family in Paris, Texas where Billy spent all of his professional life. He was an outstanding surgeon and citizen, contributing leadership to the community and documenting many historical features of the area. Billy passed away about two years ago.

Starting my senior year with more time and plans to marry after graduation, I became more serious about the future. I think that evolution in thought is called maturity. I wasn't dating any more and focused on doing well in school. I had my job at the ENT hospital and felt I was carrying a bit more of the cost of my education. Proof of all of that came near the end of my senior year when I was ranked #6 in my class academically. My grades were certainly improving as I acquired more clinical skills working with instructors and live patients. I knew I was in the right field.

Part of our senior year involved being farmed out to charity hospitals in smaller communities such as Pineville, where we could be more involved in patient care and surgical procedures. I thrived in this atmosphere and as a consequence made a very high grade in surgery.

As a senior, it was my time to be in the Bull Pen with Dr. Ochsner. Fortunately, I was able to recognize the classic appearance of a woman with Cushing's Syndrome. These people are moon-faced, have high blood pressure, stretch marks on their skin from rapid weight gain, and tend toward truncal obesity. I was very happy that my case for Dr. Ochsner was not one of the more mysterious entities.

All graduating seniors had to write a thesis during their senior year, and the subject required Dr. Burch's approval. I started a research program to check the levels of sulfa in a rabbit's eye chamber after different doses of the medicine. Research activity was not my thing. The rabbits and I were not real good friends, and I went to Dr. Burch and told him the project was a disaster. I spoke to him about my love for the history of medicine and particularly for the life story of one of the greatest physicians who ever lived, Dr. William Osler. This Canadian went to medical school at McGill University. He was later chosen to be Professor of Medicine at the University of Pennsylvania. His powers of observation and his energy allowed him to write a textbook of medicine that proved to be the Bible for medical people of the early 20th century. His next move was to Johns Hopkins where he became Professor of Medicine in that prestigious University. Later he became Professor of Medicine at Oxford University in England and ultimately was knighted by the Queen and was known from then on as Sir William Osler. He married late in life, and he and his wife had one son whom they adored. Osler suffered mightily when that young man was killed in battle in World War I. Knowing how much I loved the biography of Osler by the distinguished father of American Neurosurgery, Harvey Cushing,

Sarah gave me a specially published, two volume gold-bound issue of that great book. It is one of my treasures. I have since given the two volumes to my grandson, Brandon Allen Quinn, who aspires to attend medical school. I hope Dr. Osler's life will be an inspiration to Brandon as it was to me.

The Christmas holidays came none too soon, and I was happy to be on my way home to be with my love and our families. Life was good. Sarah was thriving as a teacher and my academic life was the best it had ever been.

The year 1953 would be big in the Allen, Ferris and McCutchon families. Two weddings, two MD degrees and internships: Denver General for me and Philadelphia General for Jimmy. There was a high level of anticipation and excitement all around as we scheduled our wedding for June 12th and Jeanne and Jimmy planned theirs for June 8th. The ten days between graduation and our wedding were jam packed with action, and I think a real stress on my parents, particularly my mother who realized both of her children would be out of her nest within four days.

Both weddings were at the beautiful Corpus Christi Cathedral. Father Anthony Goegele had been transferred to George West, but he was allowed to come to the Cathedral to marry us. Sarah's brother, Frank C. Allen, III, was our best man. Grover, Buddy, Rex and Harry Stuth were all in the wedding party. Jeanne & Jimmy were already on their honeymoon and headed for Philadelphia for Jim's internship. Life was good for the four of us.

I did not recognize how difficult this time was for my mother. As I have mentioned before, the traumatic event of watching her father, sister and her friend drown would subconsciously affect every thought and action she would have or take for the rest of her life. Today we know this condition as post-traumatic stress syndrome. She also lost a pregnancy between my birth and my sister Jeanne. Now her son and daughter would primarily belong to two other people, and it happened within the space of four days.

It was too difficult for her to process and indeed as we left the Cathedral to the applause of other family and friends and the joyous and thunderous music of the mighty organ, she collapsed and had to be taken to the hospital.

We had a great reception with dancing and spirits. Our getaway car was safely hidden in a neighborhood garage. Sarah threw the bouquet and I bravely removed the garter and tossed it to some poor soul.

Frank III had hidden our car in the neighbor's garage and was waiting in front for us to safely leave the reception. However, we were surrounded by "our friends" and chained together and a padlock applied. So our first destination was a service station where we were able to secure a bolt cutter and remove the chain. From there we went to Spohn Hospital where my mother had been admitted in her state of collapse to tell her goodbye and assure her of our prayers. I think that later evidence actually showed that she had a mild heart attack during the event. Sarah and I both regret that she had to go through all of that; however, our union would bring her much joy in the future and many beautiful grandchildren to shower her with love.

We dropped Frank III at the Allen home and thanked him profusely for being a faithful best man and protecting our getaway. Late in the night, we headed north for San Antonio, Hunt Texas, and my uncle's cabin on the Guadalupe. By the time we got to Boerne, I was very drowsy and we stopped for coffee. We were just about fifty miles from our destination. The coffee was good and perked me up. When I reached in my pocket for money to pay the bill, I felt something different. When I brought it out to see what it was – behold - the key to the padlock on the chain that bound us together. We had wasted a lot of time and effort looking for a chain cutter. We hope those rascals were satisfied with their wedding mischief.

I had no trouble finding my Uncle's cabin. We made quick

work of unpacking essentials, donned our honeymoon pajamas and nightgown and went to sleep in each other's arms. It was the beginning of a sixty-year adventure that would blossom and grow as this story will testify. We were an extremely happy couple of newlyweds.

After three days at the cabin we headed for George West, Texas where Father Anthony baptized Sarah into the Catholic faith, something which made us both very happy. He then took her to Three Rivers, where another priest heard her first Confession. That evening at the rectory, Father Anthony prepared one of his famous lasagna dinners with good red wine, and we celebrated this wonderful beginning and looked forward to her first reception of the Holy Eucharist the following morning. She seemed so much at peace with her union with me and with Holy Mother the Church. We felt so much grace pouring into our hearts.

After Mass and breakfast with Father Anthony, we headed for Garner Park where we floated in the crystal clear water of the Frio River and spent the night in one of their guest cabins.

The next day found us driving to Red River, New Mexico. The mountainous country was very beautiful, and we decided to check in there for the night. We must have looked pretty young because the desk clerk asked our ages before she would sign us up for a room. She also found out that I was a doctor and tried to get me to see a hotel guest who was ailing. I sympathized but told her I had no license to practice medicine in New Mexico.

The next day we headed for Santa Fe. As we went over the pass, our radiator boiled over in the thin air of high altitude, and we took time to let things cool down and admired the beauty of the mountains. Our next stop was Roswell, where we visited Colonel and Mrs. Lusk, old and dear friends of Sarah's parents. Colonel Lusk had been superintendent of the New Mexico Military Institute where Sarah's dad, uncle and brother had attended school and junior college. Sally Talley also lived there but was out of town at the time. We then headed for Raton Pass and entered Colorado, with Denver in our sights and our home base for the next year.

We arrived at the home of Aunt Peg and Uncle Mike Wytias, welcomed with open arms, lots of warmth and a family that thrived on activity, fun, song, fishing and camping. Charlotte, Chuck, and Susie were the happy cousins in this group. Aunt Peg had found us a garage apartment just about 3 blocks from their home on Belmont Street. It was perfect except for the mouse that ran across the floor and chased Sarah into the bathroom as fast as she could go.

Rex Ramsay was our first visitor at our new apartment home. He had come to town to start his internship at Colorado General Hospital, the main teaching hospital for the University of Colorado-School of Medicine. We were so happy to have him in the same city with us. We would be available to treat his lovesick blues for Tee Patrick who he sadly had to leave in New Orleans. Buddy Patrick had gone to San Francisco General Hospital, so we wouldn't see him for some time although we did correspond a couple of times and knew he was happy and doing well as an intern there.

Grover, Paul Anderson, and I all showed up for our first orientation meeting at Denver General Hospital to find that we would be working 24 hour shifts every other night and some weekends for the next six months. Grover and I would go to General Rose Memorial Hospital for the second six months, and Paul would stay at Denver General for the entire year. We also met Jim and Julie Wise, Coloradoans, and Sydney and Louis Tatom who came from Duke University-School of Medicine, as fellow interns. Lou Tatom was the only intern without an M.D. behind his name because Duke would not award the Doctor of Medicine degree until completion of an accredited internship.

Lou and Sydney became close friends with Sarah and me, and

we made a few weekend trips together for skiing and relaxing. Sometime around November of that year, Denver General placed a moratorium on skiing for the House Staff because so many of them were missing work and wearing casts or slowed down by crutches due to injuries sustained while skiing.

I attained some notoriety as an intern when my supervising resident admitted an elderly male to the hospital with a diagnosis of Guillain-Barré syndrome. This syndrome occurs in patients whose immune system reacts to an offending virus or other insult, such as immunization, by attacking the nerves in the feet and legs and may progressively ascend to the upper body and even the brain. Due to lack of a good history, this was a plausible diagnosis. I proceeded with the usual format - examining the head, eyes, ears, nose and throat which all seemed to be within normal limits. When I placed my hand behind his neck to check for stiffness, I felt a sensation of crepitus. There are many physical examination moments when the word crepitus is applicable, such as applied to crackles in the lungs with pneumonia. However, crepitus in this situation applied to irregular edges of broken bones grating against each other. Could the paralysis of all four limbs in this unfortunate individual be associated with a broken neck? Undoubtedly so! I stabilized his neck with sandbags and sent him off to X-ray and a look at the cervical spine.

Later, when I talked with persons who knew the patient, they said he had accidentally fallen down some stairs but didn't seem to have any serious injury. When swelling around the fracture set in and placed pressure on the spinal cord, paralysis began and proceeded rapidly. He would remain a quadriplegic the rest of his life. Emergency ambulance crews today have all sorts of neck immobilization supports to stabilize the cervical spine and prevent tragedies such as this. They use them generously at the slightest indication of neck trauma.

When I did my surgery rotation as an intern at Denver General I worked under the supervision of a young first year resident by the name of Bud Wilson.

I had never worked with an individual so energetic, meticulous, and who loved his work so much. He did everything with energy, a smile and compassion for his patient. Furthermore, he cured patients quickly when surgery was the treatment of choice. He made me think I could be a surgeon, and I applied for one of the top surgical residencies in the country at Parkland Memorial Hospital in Dallas, Texas. I wrote Dr. Ochsner for a recommendation. It must have been a glowing one because I received a phone call from Ben J. Wilson, Chairman of the Department of Surgery, and Chief of the Surgery Service at Parkland. Dr. Wilson said he had never accepted a resident without a personal interview, but based on my transcript and the letter from Dr. Ochsner I would not have to interrupt my training in Denver, to journey to Dallas. I was elated and felt I was on the correct path for the future.

Sarah was doing well teaching 4th grade on split session with Miss Fulton, a spinster who always wore a smock. Schools were crowded with baby boomers since the end of World War II, all of the soldiers coming home, marrying and becoming fathers.

Sarah's mother was born and raised in Denver. Unfortunately, she developed active rheumatoid arthritis as a young student at the University of Denver. All the currently known treatments failed to relieve her, and the doctor advised her to move to a warmer climate. Sarah's grandmother was Jane Armitage Crosby before she married Charles Josiah Taylor. She had a cousin in Corpus Christi, Texas by the name of Roxie Armitage who was married to a banker named Billy Sheffield. The Sheffield's didn't have any children and offered to have Betty Taylor come and live with them. The 'S' on our set of silverware is for Sheffield. The silver service was a gift to Sarah's mother, Betty Taylor, who bequeathed it to Sarah Jane.

Peg and Mike Wytias, and their four children, Charlotte, Susie, Chuck, and Betty Jane, had us over often. They took us camping in September to the mountains where our pup tent was covered with ice by morning. The only way we kept warm was to put one sleeping bag inside the other and both crawl into the inside bag. We believed in warmth and togetherness.

Mike Wytias and Sarah's uncle Chuck Taylor owned and operated a creamery in Denver. Chuck and Chris had one daughter, Christine. Betty's oldest sister, Jane Taylor, and her husband, John Pace, had one daughter, Nora Jane. Sarah's Uncle Jack Taylor and his wife Bonnie were great singers and performed with the Denver Opera. They had two sons, Johnny and Stan. We had plenty of family support in our first year of marriage.

In spite of this, we really wanted to get home to Corpus Christi and to our families for the holidays. Snow was heavy and we had to put chains on the tires to get out of Colorado. After Raton Pass, we chugged through northern New Mexico and crossed the border, headed for Dumas. I was singing one of my dad's old songs, "I'm a Ding Dong Daddy from Dumas!" when a sudden percussion instrument joined the song as the trusted old '49 Ford threw a rod, and we rolled to a stop, homeless in the High Plains. We contacted family, caught a bus to Amarillo, and a train to Corpus Christi. Thank God for loving family support. There was lots of hugging and kissing at the train station from a group that would always be a powerful magnet drawing us to our roots. Christmas and the birth of the Christ child would always be a very special time in the lives of our family.

We headed back to Denver in order to make our move to General Rose Memorial Hospital for the last half of our internship. We picked up our repaired car in Dalhart, courtesy of Sarah's family, and headed for General Rose. One advantage we gained at Rose was room and board in the hospital at no cost to us. We had one large room with a connecting bath where we would spend the next six months and save lots of money. With me earning only $50 monthly and Sarah's teaching salary at $250 monthly, that reduction in cost of living made a big difference in our checking account.

The timing was perfect because Sarah told me she missed her period for early February. She visited the doctor and he confirmed early pregnancy. When she gave me the news, I was so excited I ran a red light on Colfax and was given a ticket we could ill-afford. Fortunately, I went to court and a softhearted judge analyzed our plight and forgave the fine. God bless him forever.

At Rose, Grover and I had a view of the private practice of medicine, surgery and Obstetrics. It was a real pleasure to see these fine men fulfilling their roles in society and caring for a large segment of the American scene. They were well dressed, polite and willing to share their knowledge with the interns.

General Maurice Rose was a Jewish American for whom the hospital was named. He was considered a war hero. Most of the medical staff were Jewish doctors and, as is usually the case, were at the top of their profession. They were good and willing teachers, and I've always been thankful for my training there.

As June approached, we organized for our trip to Dallas and residency training. Grover would head for Pineville and spend some time in the family practice residency program. He was waiting for the Air Force to call him to active duty for his two years of obligated service at Yuma Air Force Base (AFB). Buddy Patrick also went to Pineville and started a family practice residency. Paul and Joan Anderson served their two years of obligated service at Geiger Field in Spokane, Washington. Paul's sister Phyllis also married a classmate of ours, George Olive from Crenshaw County, Alabama. George's assignment was Victoria AFB in South Texas. Because of our age and our deferments, we all had 2 years of active duty to give our country. Rex Ramsay went to work as a prison doctor in Florida and ended up in a

Pediatric residency at Jackson Memorial in Miami.

My first year as a surgery resident at Parkland did not go well. I was really enjoying my venture into the surgical world until we were called upon to go to McKinney VA hospital to work with polio patients in iron lungs. About ten days later, I was having lunch With Dr. Wilson and the chief resident, and I attempted to pour them a glass of tea. I couldn't lift the pitcher with my left arm. I was dumbfounded at this weakness. I did not feel ill, but I lacked energy. I attributed that symptom to our long work hours. Dr. Wilson called the chief medical resident who examined me, did a spinal tap, and made a diagnosis of acute poliomyelitis. I was hospitalized at the old Parkland Hospital and taken off the surgical rotation.

Catherine Mary Ferris, our first born, and Sarah were both still in St. Paul's Hospital. Both our mothers came from Corpus Christi to be with Sarah and the baby, both of whom were doing fine. I was kept in the hospital until the period of contagion was over and then allowed to come home. The grandmothers went home and I began physical therapy at Baylor Hospital to regain as much strength in my left shoulder as possible. The therapists used a perfumed skin cream for massage treatment, and each day Sarah was becoming more seriously concerned that I was getting more than physical therapy at Baylor. She finally confronted me about her suspicion and I was able to allay her anxiety.

I was allowed to return to work on the pathology service with Dr. P. O'B. Montgomery. This assignment would be light and gave me a chance to gain some strength. I knew I would never be a pathologist because I'm colorblind and the stains on the slides never seemed to match what the other doctors saw at our conferences. I was frustrated. Dr. Wilson called me in for a discussion about my future training and thought I should consider entering a radiology program. I told him I was a people person and wanted to interact with patients as my Uncle David had done.

I told him I thought I'd better go home and wait for my call to active duty and find a part time job in the interim. He agreed with the plan and released me from my contract.

About that time a beautiful thing happened. Mama Ferris, called from Austin, and said that she wanted to fly to Dallas, and see her new great-grandbaby, Catherine Mary Ferris. Sarah and I were ecstatic to think that the matriarch of my dad's family would make that trip by herself to see our new daughter. This grand Lebanese-American woman who had lived in two mansions was coming to stay with us in our low rent housing project. She wanted to spend time with her newest great-grandchild. She came bearing gifts. The first was a little stuffed monkey doll that Aunt Anna had made a few months before but had not sent because Mama Ferris feared the baby would look like a monkey if Sarah saw it before Catherine was born! The second gift was an electric meat grinder with the admonition to personally choose from the butcher high quality lamb, beef and pork, and always grind it three times. She lovingly wanted to make it easy for Sarah to keep high standards in the preparation of the baby's food.

Mama Ferris stayed with us for three days and was such a joy with her Old Country ways. Her love was all encompassing. How blessed we were. In her waning years, she lived in a beautiful care-giving private home in Austin, and we always visited her on our trips there. She was laid to rest after a beautiful funeral Mass at St. Mary's Cathedral in downtown Austin. I was so proud to be there.

While we were still in Dallas, my good friend, Jack Schneider announced that he was marrying Ellie Luckett from New Braunfels, Sweetheart of the University of Texas. He wanted us to be in the wedding party, so we headed to Austin for the festivities. Sarah's brother, Frank III, had married Mary Jo Bader while he was at Fort Knox, Kentucky. They were living in Austin at this time and took care of baby Catherine while we celebrated at the pre- and post-nuptial festivities. The wedding was a grand affair and began a long friendship between the Schneider and Ferris families. We spent several Summers in the Schneider vacation home on Lake Travis with all of our family together. We recently spent a weekend with Jack & Ellie in their condominium at Carencia in South Austin. We made a sentimental visit to their home on Lake Travis and relived the joys of our family vacations there. Ellie is enduring Parkinson problems but meets every challenge with the dignity and the courage that has characterized her life.

When we left Dallas and returned to Corpus Christi, October 1954, I knew I had to find some temporary gainful employment for the next ten months until called to active duty in the Air Force. Somehow I heard about a possibility at the Kingsville Clinic, where I had started my pre-med studies at Texas A & I. I went over to investigate and after several interviews with the doctor partners was offered a primary care position with the understanding that I would be leaving for active duty after June 30, 1956. The clinic had a multi-disciplinary medical staff composed of Earl Gaston in surgery, Chester Dunn in Pediatrics, Heywood Walling in Obstetrics-Gynecology, Newell Boyd in primary care, and Russell Scales in Internal Medicine. I enjoyed working with them, and I think I fulfilled their expectations for more availability and more income. The experience gave me the opportunity to have an inside look at private practice. It, at least, put some groceries on the table for my little family, and I did not feel so poverty stricken. We lived in an apartment complex near the Naval Air Station. We became friends with Navy doctors John Eisenlohr and his wife Marty, and Phil Snodgrass and his wife. The Eisenlohr's ended up in Dallas in ophthalmology, and Phil went on to be a Professor of Medicine in Iowa City. Both men were very bright doctors.

Dr. Walling also delivered our second child, John A. Ferris, III, on September 27th, after just a short time in Kingsville.

Kingsville was more than just a town to Sarah. Her family roots ran very deep there. Her granddad, Frank C. Allen, Sr., and his younger brother, Clyde Allen went into business there in 1908. They established a furniture store that included a funeral parlor. That furniture store stayed in business 99 years, finally closing in 2007. After Uncle Clyde's death, Clyde, Jr. and his wife Judy managed the store. Clyde, Jr., turned out to be a very astute businessman and successfully managed that store until it closed at the completion of its 99th year in business. All the relatives bought furniture there and Clyde, Jr. would look out the window from time to time and groan, "Here comes another relative!" In spite of this adversity, he and Judy were very successful and made many relatives very happy. They are enjoying retirement and visiting their grandchildren. Clyde, Jr. served on the Board of the Kleberg National Bank in Kingsville for many years and, in fact, also served as the bank's President for a time.

August of 1956 came too soon and I reported for active duty at the Air Force Orientation program in Montgomery, Alabama. I soon learned I would be assigned to the Air Force Hospital at Clark AFB in the Philippines. Sarah was 8 months into her third pregnancy, and I would be leaving her and our three babies behind with the possibility that my family might join me if all went well.

After a long and tiring flight that included stops in Hawaii and Wake Island, I arrived at Clark AFB to meet my new roommate, Dr. James Cassidy, a very bright internist from Oak Park, Illinois. Jim was a good Irish Catholic with a great wife, Nan, who would eventually bear him eight beautiful children. Joe and Cathy Wesp, another fine Catholic family with eight children, was an Obstetrician and Gynecologist in the regular Air Force.

We made great friendships there with Pediatrician John Moore, his wife, Pauline, and their two boys; Bob Kellum and his wife, Marilyn; and later Art and Rosemary Baue, from the St. Louis area who went on to the fame I previously described. Art had all the qualifications of a great surgeon. He was very bright, studied hard, and not the least bit timid in undertaking procedures in surgery, even when his Chief was away. The gap between his knowledge and ability and my own was like the Grand Canyon. I had great admiration for him and realized how inadequate my qualifications were as a surgeon. I described his illustrious career earlier in this book.

Meanwhile back home, Christopher Allen Ferris was born on October 18, 1956. Sarah's dad took her to the hospital and was quite puffed up with pride when he was mistaken as being the baby's father. Sarah had a difficult and painful labor, however, she and the baby did well and all of us celebrated with a long distance phone call via the Pacific cable. What a contrast with today's cellular phone calls, and the old lag in speech transmission traveling 1800 miles in a cable!

I spent most of my time assisting in surgery and seeing patients in the surgery outpatient clinic. Our work was routine, except for two cases that I distinctly remember. At that time, cardiac resuscitation was in its embryonic form. It had come to pass that the current treatment for cardiac arrest in a patient who had a chance of viability was to open the chest and manually squeeze the heart with one's hand, but only if all other mechanical and injectable medications failed.

It so happened that I was caught on the ward one day with that exact situation. The unfortunate patient was a middle-aged man on the surgery service who had a cardiac arrest and the usual resuscitative medications failed. No senior surgeons were available and the buck stopped with me. I asked for the emergency surgical kit and opened his chest with an intercostal incision and mechanically massaged his heart with my gloved hand. I did not want to be there, but I was. The emergency resuscitation failed as his heart refused to start again. I am so thankful that cardiac resuscitation has progressed to a more civilized state. We have slowly learned what chest compression and mouth-to-mouth respiratory assistance can do, as well as portable defibrillators, when appropriate. Heart attacks these days are much less frequent because we have learned how to control the risk factors of smoking, high blood pressure, high cholesterol, and sugar. I call these four risk factors the four Horsemen of the Apocalypse. If these are well controlled, it is very unlikely that coronary disease will take the life of the patient.

My second memory involved the loss of a teenage baseball player who was beaned by an errant pitch. He died from an epidural hemorrhage that no one recognized as such until it was too late. It is true that one never forgets the hurt of failures while multiple successes are just part of the routine day.

As Thanksgiving and the Christmas holidays approached, I was looking forward to seeing the family. I had received permission to bring Sarah and the three children overseas to be with me for the rest of my tour. Housing was unavailable on the base at the time, and we would have to live in Angeles, a small town very near the base. We were lonesome and figured the inconvenience would be worth the effort.

My flight to California, in a Lockheed Constellation, involved refueling stops in Guam and Hawaii and was uneventful. I flew commercial from California to Corpus Christi. Sarah was in church when I arrived, and I immediately went to St. Patrick's and sat down beside her. We were two of the happiest people one can imagine.

Christmas with both families was wonderful. Our own little family was growing with Catherine Mary two years of old, John III one year old and now Christopher Allen at six weeks. We spent some busy days getting ready to transport the entire little family to the Philippines. We flew to San Francisco where we boarded a US president liner for the long trip across the Pacific. We put the two toddlers on a leash and of course carried the baby. Just before departure, I was standing at the ship railing waving to people on the dock and became seasick before we had ever cast off. I pictured myself being seasick for two and a half weeks, but fortunately, I never felt that way again.

We had a nice stateroom that held all five of us quite comfortably. We took all three of our daily meals in the Captain's dining room. We all had to be properly dressed, including the children. It was like going out to eat three times a day. The food was excellent and the children thought it was so much fun to go to dinner.

We heard stories about small children falling overboard, so we always kept them on a leash under our wary eyes. They often played on the deck with their toys and seemed to enjoy the trip. Fortunately we all stayed well. The adventure was new to all of us as we had never experienced sailing the ocean.

When we arrived in the Philippines, we had no housing on the base for us. We moved into a small, newly built bungalow in Balibago. We had two bedrooms and a bath. The bathroom and the kitchen had kerosene stoves for cooking and warmth. Sarah mastered the art of cooking with kerosene. She also mastered the art of staying alone with the babies when I had night duty at the hospital. She had heard stories of babies being stolen, particularly the blondes and fair skinned children like Christopher. If I was not a home at night, she could not sleep for fear of losing a child. She started smoking to stay awake at night. This really upset me because of all the morbidity associated with smoking. I promised to do anything in the world for her if she'd quit smoking. She complied and has never smoked again.

Mitchell Young, from Texarkana, was a young physician inducted to active duty in Montgomery at the same time I was. His assignment was Bangkok, Thailand where he ran a dispensary that would look after the health problems of all United States personnel in the area. I was assigned to take over his duty while he went on leave. Mitchell and Donna Young had married just before he went overseas. I will mention him once again when we count children.

My flight to Thailand is one etched deeply into my memory as one I shall never forget. As we flew over the Strait of Luzon toward Formosa (now Taiwan), we encountered the most violent storm one could imagine. Our aircraft was tossed about so violently that both pilots were vomiting. I felt we were doomed and I was fervently praying my rosary. Somehow, we miraculously survived that storm, and once again, I gave thanks to our Blessed Lady for her succor in our time of need.

Once safely in Thailand, I reported to my work site which was a small medical clinic with two emergency beds and two examining rooms with nursing and administrative help. Really sick or injured people had to be referred to local medical facilities or flown out to military hospitals such as Clark or Japan.

My meals and quarters were in a large home run by a Thai lady who gave us only authentic Thai food. I tired of it very quickly, but I didn't have much choice. I had plenty of time for sightseeing, and I visited rural areas and learned how the locals farmed. There seemed to be Temples everywhere and many young monks. The business sections of Bangkok were overrun with cyclists balancing their wares on their heads while trying to keep from being run over by cars darting everywhere. The entire hubbub was unappealing to me, and I was ready to get back to Clark AFB and my family. My most treasured memory was buying a beautiful black star sapphire ring to present to Sarah on my return home. She still wears it and that makes me very happy.

Back in the Philippines, we resumed a more normal lifestyle. Base housing became available to us, and we moved into a lovely three bedroom home with a kitchen, living room, dining room and separate quarters for the house girls. We were so fortunate to find Antonina Hafalla and a few weeks later her sister Victoria. They were from Baguio City, a resort town in the mountains where it was cool and the odor of pine trees was in the air. It reminded me of Colorado. The Air Force had a Rest and Recreation facility there called Camp John Hay. Oh, how we loved to go there! They had a beautiful and challenging golf course that we loved to play. I'll never forget the day Sarah and I were playing this 4 par uphill hole, and she hit a beautiful drive to the middle of the fairway. She pulled out her 3 wood and knocked it 12 feet from pin. Then with complete nonchalance, she putted the ball home for a natural birdie. I was really impressed, and it seemed like no big deal to her!

Antonina and Victoria's brother was the Pro at the Camp John Hay Golf course so we always felt like special guests when we were there. After we were back in the States, we received a phone call from Antonina one day saying she had come to America with a military family returning from Clark. She wanted to say hello and find out how the children were doing. We had tried to bring Antonina and Victoria home with us but could not make arrangements to do so. Apparently her sponsoring family knew the right steps to accomplish her visa. We never heard from her again. We really loved her and wished we could have seen her, but it didn't work out. She cared so much about our children.

John and Pauline Moore, Bob and Miriam Kellum, and Sarah and I planned a trip to Hong Kong and Japan. The men would fly military and the girls would go commercially. We met in Hong Kong for sightseeing, shopping and dining. We ordered the usual made-to-measure clothes and some inexpensive jewelry. We felt like we had hit the big time. From there we went on to Japan where we rode the trains, enjoyed Japanese cuisine, and saw the temples; but best of all, Sarah and I rented two bicycles and took off through the Japanese countryside in the shadow of Fuji. We stopped at a little country store and enjoyed drinks and snacks and rode until we found a unique little motel composed of individual tepee-like cabins that made the setting look like an Indian campground. I would like to say we checked in for the night, but alas, we promised the bicycles back by dark and had to hit the road and then find our way back to our hotel. With this wonderful trip behind us, the girls caught their commercial flight home and the guys went back to the base and caught a ride back to Clark. It was a great and enlightening week for all of us. Needless to say our little ones and our house girls were glad to see us again.

We spent the Christmas holidays at Camp John Hay which made the season delightfully Christmas. The children were thriving and receiving lots of attention from the house girls and Sarah. I loved to be with them in the evening, and we began a tradition of family prayers and bedtime stories. We returned home to Clark after Christmas, and Sarah's fourth pregnancy was in its 34th week. She was doing well and the new baby was kicking.

On the night of February 19, 1958, we were having a nice quiet family supper when a startled look came over Sarah's face followed by the words "my water broke"! I gave Joe Wesp a call and he said, "meet me at the hospital". Two hours later we had another beautiful baby girl, and so began the earthly life of Martha Anne Ferris, affectionately known to all as Tita. It just so happens that as I am writing this family history, she appeared at our doorstep this very night, 55 years later and brought us a wonderful shrimp and rice supper. She and her husband Bill Adams have showered us with love and have opened their home to us when we can no longer make it on our own. What if we had said three children are all we can afford and thus have missed knowing and loving this beautiful person. It takes a leap of faith to do such things and wiser people than I call it irresponsible. I call it the Gift of Faith, taught to me by my parents, the nuns and the priests, who shepherded me through high school. After high school I was in state and nonsectarian colleges and universities, but the foundation for faith was already in place.

Time in the Philippines was drawing to a close, and I would soon be released from Active Duty and be able to begin life as a civilian. We had a choice to fly home or go by boat. We were uneasy about flying across the Pacific with four small children so we elected another cruise. This time we were assigned a cabin in the lower deck with no porthole and the trip wasn't as much fun as it was going over. We had a chance to sightsee in Hawaii and that was fun; that is, as much fun as anyone could have with four toddlers. It wasn't too long before we were very close to California and in the densest fog I had ever seen. We were approaching San Francisco, and you could not see your hand in front of your face. When we finally recovered from being frightened by ear shattering foghorns and broke into clear weather, we saw one of the most beautiful symbols of America - The Golden Gate Bridge! A feeling of warmth surged through our souls as we felt the depth of our love for America as we sailed under her giant span. We gave thanks for the courageous men and women who gave their lives to keep us free.

We rented a station wagon at the ship terminal and headed for Travis Air Force Base to be officially discharged from active duty, though I would remain in the Air Force Reserve. The process took the rest of our day so it was dark when we headed for the San Francisco airport to catch our plane to Corpus Christi. I was a bit drowsy and the car was weaving somewhat. A State Highway Patrol officer pulled me over and inquired as to my sobriety. He believed my story when he saw the little ones asleep in the back. He wisely advised me to pull over and get some sleep and protect the precious cargo I was carrying.

When we landed in Corpus Christi, you would have thought the President was coming to town. Both sets of grandparents and all the aunts, uncles and cousins were lined up at the exit gate to welcome us home. In those days of a simpler life, the welcome party could get very close to the plane. We could see them all through our plane windows. I can't tell you how good those loving faces looked after not seeing them for a year and a half. It was truly a good day.

Both sets of grandparent were so anxious to get to know the grandchildren that we alternated spending the night with one and then the other. Life was good. Catherine became "Kaki"; Johnny became "Bubbie"; Chris was spared a nickname; and eventually Martha Anne became "Tita".

One evening around the table Bubbie was babbling to Sarah and I said "sounds like he's speaking Tagalog", and Kaki quickly retorted, "No! He's speaking to Mama!" Her mind has always been so quick. She is happily married to Rick Cole, a former high school boyfriend. Her first marriage to Eduardo Lapaz brought us four beautiful grandchildren. Lucia Camille who is in graduate school; Laura Michelle who is in the business world of dentistry; Diego Martin who has found it difficult to deal with the reality understood by ordinary men. I'm sure he will one day surprise us all by blossoming into some sort of genius. Finally there is Sarah Isabelle, who graduated from high school this year number 6 in a class of 1200. She will be going to Oklahoma City University to pursue the study of Voice and Drama. I think she has her eye on Broadway. She is a gifted student of voice and will someday share her talent with the world of music.

Here we are in the States again, released from active duty, biding our time with our families in Corpus Christi, and the reality that we have 4 small children and no income hits us. I had decided that I better get to work and that my family need not suffer the privation of a resident's income. A local physician suggested I go see Dr. Voss in Odem, a small town just about 22 miles from Corpus Christi. He was a fine man doing good primary care in a small town, but his practice was in the shadow of Corpus Christi and too close to home. Then I went to meet Dr. Elmo Muecke in Three Rivers, and I liked him very much but things still didn't seem to be just what I wanted. For some reason my thoughts drifted to the Rio Grande Valley, a place I knew little about. My folks occasionally went down there to get away from their routine, and I knew my mother loved the beauty and fragrance of the citrus in bloom. I had been there only twice to play football against Mercedes High School and basketball against St. Joseph Academy in Brownsville. Those night games didn't let me get a look at the scenery. We always went across the border into Mexico, after the games to have dinner and shop for trinkets and gifts to take home. One of the big deals was to buy Chanel No.5 perfume at a big discount and give it to one's girlfriend. At the time I didn't have a girlfriend, but I had my eye on Ginger Boyd, a beautiful brunette with fair skin and very dark eyebrows. I think we danced once but I never dated her. I heard she had a very steady boyfriend. Anyway, I gathered enough nerve to knock on her door one evening and presented her with the prize bottle of Chanel No. 5. She gave me a quizzical look, said thank you, took the perfume and shut the door! I'm sure she thought I was from Loony Tunes.

I told Sarah I wanted to check out the Valley as a possible practice location. One of Dad's attorney friends suggested I look up John Quincy Adams, an attorney in Harlingen. I was referred to his young associate, Martin P. Ferrero, who was very cordial and thought I would do well. He ultimately became my patient and I, his client. Martin recently passed away after a long and debilitating illness. Martin suggested that I visit Bob Scoggins, a young CPA who practiced in Harlingen but lived near Rio Hondo, a very small community seven miles east of Harlingen. The Port of Harlingen was actually in Rio Hondo, and it connected the Arroyo Colorado with the Intracoastal Waterway. Barges bearing fuel, fertilizers, cotton, and other bulk necessities were frequent visitors supplying the Valley's needs for these commodities or exporting goods produced in the Valley.

Bob Scoggins wanted me to meet Al and Ralph Roiz, who, with their father, ran a small drug store in Rio Hondo. The sons were pharmacists and knew a great deal about medicine in the area. Valley Baptist Hospital had just constructed a new 150 bed hospital on the east side of Harlingen that was an easy ten minute commute to Rio Hondo and no traffic; actually a country boy's dream! Office space was available on Main Street just across the street from the drug store. It was a Saturday afternoon in August and the town was bulging with braceros, legal Mexican farm laborers brought in for the cotton harvest. They were covered by insurance that would pay $2.00 for an office visit. They, of course, had all the common maladies of the human race as well as frequent minor injuries associated with their work, so I would begin to make a living and pay expenses right away.

My criterion for a practice location was gradually being met. Small town, people in need, good hospital within seven miles, independence from burdens of salary and/or partnership, two fine men in the pharmacy profession to work with; it all seemed right and I decided Rio Hondo, Texas was about to get a new doctor.

When I brought my dad down to show him the town, the office, and the hospital, he didn't say much. I think he was disappointed as I'm sure he and Mom would have enjoyed having their grandchildren closer to them and seeing us more often. I hope they forgave our selfishness in trying to lead a different style of life. At least they had Jimmy and Jeanne and their little ones to keep them company. We resolved to visit both our families often since it was only a two and a half hour drive to Corpus Christi. We would also encourage both families to visit us often.

I applied to Valley Baptist Hospital for staff privileges and was given a provisional acceptance. If I did well during the two-year observation, I would have full staff privileges. At that time the active staff was composed of only 35 physicians. One of the leading physicians was an internist by the name of Howard Tewell. One of his patients, who lived in Rio Hondo, collapsed from a massive hemorrhage in the gastro-intestinal tract. I was called in to see him at home and realized he was in shock from blood loss. He was on Coumadin, an anticoagulant still used extensively today. I carried intravenous fluids in my doctor bag, and I was able to start fluids on him while someone else was calling the

84

ambulance. I had vitamin K in my bag and injected the antidote for Coumadin overdose while the patient was still on the floor. He arrived safely in the emergency room where Dr.Tewell awaited him and took over his care, duly impressed by the new doctor in the small town of Rio Hondo.

Another physician who befriended me early on was Joe Louis "Tops" Moet. He was an outstanding general practitioner with an office in La Feria, seven miles west of Harlingen. He was in the Navy during World War II and had lots of experience in war zones. He was very gracious in helping me learn the ropes as I was integrated into the medical community. I valued him as a mentor and gracious colleague. He made me feel very comfortable at Valley Baptist.

In October of 1958, the Rio Grande Valley was being deluged with rain and our floodway was taking on the excess water. Dr. Moet and his friend Tom Winn decided to go to Mercedes and check on some goats they had grazing in the floodway. They invited their wives to go along in the back seat of Tom's Thunderbird. It was a dark night as they approached old Highway 83 to turn left and head for Mercedes. As they pulled out onto Highway 83, they were broadsided by a sheriff's deputy who was pursuing another vehicle with his headlights off. Dr. Moet and Tom Winn were killed instantly and the wives suffered multiple fractures but survived.

I felt terrible about the tragedy, and in order to help Martha Moet preserve the value of Top's practice, I started going to his office in the afternoon three times a week to see his patients. His brother, Dr. John Allen Moet, who practiced in Orange Grove, arranged a sale of one half of the building to me and a chance to take on a much bigger practice than I had in Rio Hondo. I signed a note for $20,000. On January 1, 1959, I moved my practice to La Feria. Sarah and I purchased a comfortable old 3-bedroom home on West and Primrose, with a garage and utility room attached, for $12,500. It had a nice yard where the children could play. Sarah and our parents were delighted to see us become a bit more secure. Both of our families came to see us occasionally and we in turn made visits to Corpus Christi. Life was good!

Jackie Eddleblute, an RN, went to work for me in the office. Her husband Dana, was a building contractor, and we became good friends. Alma Lightsey tended to appointments and kept the books.

A little history of medical practice in the area is in order. In the late thirties, Nazism was on the rise in Germany. Adolph Hitler, and his philosophy of forming an Aryan race, was beginning to threaten Jews living in Germany. Heinrich Lamm was in medical school there and was doing very well. Surgical practice was very crude as it pertained to diseases of the esophagus and stomach. If one needed to look into those areas of the body, one used a long rigid metal scope that caused many perforations, tears and deaths due to infection. The patients became inexperienced sword swallowers and fell victims to perforations and infections. Heinrich's inquisitive mind envisioned the possibility of peering through a bundle of flexible glass fibers to safely navigate the curvatures of the throat and stomach. He put together a long bundle of glass fibers, bent them around a corner and placed a light bulb at one end of the fibers and a photographic plate at the other end. Sure enough, an image of the light bulb appeared on the photographic plate. This simple experiment proved that an image could be transmitted around a corner using a bundle of glass fibers. This promised to make the investigation of curving body cavities much safer. Heinrich Lamm was the first man in the world to publish this discovery in a scientific journal. Unfortunately for Heinrich, an RCA scientist had discovered the same thing, patented the discovery, then set it aside because of his interest in blossoming radio research. Heinrich never received any reward for this work except the satisfaction of revealing this discovery to the scientific world. The endoscopies of today, where doctors examine the interiors of the colon, stomach, lungs, and perform surgery, are based on these early experiments.

Heinrich and his wife, Dr. Annie Lamm, barely escaped Germany and the ravaging web of Hitler's mass executions of any Jews his storm troopers could find. The Lamm's settled in La Feria and later moved to Harlingen, where they helped many people for many years. Heinrich was an excellent surgeon, and Annie gave all his patients anesthetics and still managed to deliver over two thousand babies in her career. They left their mark on many of our Valley communities. They were inseparable and loved to dine at Arturo's restaurant in Nuevo Progresso, Mexico, a small border town just south of Mercedes and Weslaco.

The Lamm's had two very bright children, Michael and Miriam, who grew up and went to school in La Feria. Michael is a writer and publisher living in Stockton, California. Miriam was married to an ophthalmologist living in Philadelphia, but unfortunately she was widowed and has moved to California, to be closer to her children. She was recently in the Valley for her high school reunion, and I had lunch with her. Some of my colleagues and I started a memorial fund to honor the Lamm's memory, and this fund now has an untouchable principal of over $300,000, earning about $24,000 a year to award $500 to $700 scholarships to deserving students in health care professional schools. Much of the fund's growth has been due to the vision and leadership of Dr. Karl Fry, the late Dr. Tom Klug, and Drs. Max Harris, George Toland and Adela Valdez. Judy Quisenberry and her staff from the foundation do the hard work of record maintenance, application screening, and management of the fund. It not only honors the Lamm's, but also the medical and dental staff of Valley Baptist Medical Center. I also want to honor two previous administrative directors of the Lamm committee whose hard work insured its growth and fairness to applicants. Katie McCarty was our first non-physician fund manager who started us on the right track and did that work for several years. Laurie Simmons took over from

Katie and helped us manage the fund and screen the applicants carefully. All three of these fund managers have been outstanding and are in large part responsible for the fund's success. We also owe a debt of gratitude to a Baptist investment management group in Waco, which has kept our return on principal at 8% or better during some very challenging investment years when most people have looked at 1 or 2 %. The Lamm family has been very supportive and grateful for the fund honoring their parents, and the medical and dental staff at Valley Baptist can be proud of their contribution to the education of the people who support them in their daily care of the sick.

Meanwhile, back at the corner of West and Magnolia Streets in La Feria, the Ferris family was growing. Paul arrived to join the group, and we became a family with five children. We were meeting our neighbors, attending St. Francis Xavier Catholic Church just half-a-block down West Street, and starting our older children in school at St. Anthony's in Harlingen. Household help was affordable, and this fact enabled Sarah to have some time for herself and make friends with others her age and to increase the quality of her life. We made retreats and marriage encounter workshops through the Church to strengthen our love for each other.

We met many new friends who invited us to dinner and genuinely welcomed us into their businesses and homes. The children found an abundant supply of playmates and family life grew more and more interesting.

It was a little more than another year and Elizabeth Frances, named to honor her two grandmothers, joined the family circle. Now we had three girls and three boys to make a perfectly balanced group. The practice was growing in a wonderful little town at a pace that enabled me to pay our bills and enjoy the nearness of a good hospital where I could safely attend some critically sick patients. The children seemed to prosper and make friends. Sarah seemed happy, though very busy, and her circle of friends was ever widening to include the wives of my hospital colleagues.

After the Doctors Lamm left La Feria, and a couple years before I arrived, a young physician moved into their office by the name of Rudolph Hecht, M.D. He came from Mexico City where his father was a renowned entomologist. Rudy and I became very good friends and colleagues and enjoyed our common interest in medicine as well as a cordial friendship. Our wives met and enjoyed each other's company, and our children often played together. Ilse Hecht was a very special lady, and she and Sarah truly enjoyed visiting with one another. Her parents were Opa and Oma Heilbron. Her father, Fritz, started and organized the domestic duck industry in Mexico. Oma was a diminutive woman in stature but a sleeping giant at the Poker table.

One memorable day featured our Christopher sitting on a chair in a wagon, a cape around his shoulders, a hat on his head and a long stick in his hand, being pulled and fanned with large palm leaves by the other children. When Dr. Hecht inquired as to the meaning of this unusual scene, the response was "Oh! He's the Pope"! Living proof of the value of early Catholic education!

Highway 83 that spanned the Valley from east to west was a three lane killer. Dr. Lamm, God rest his soul, had three wrecks on this stretch of highway between his office and Valley Baptist Hospital while he was serving as chairman of the highway safety committee for the Texas Medical Association. We laughed a lot about that! He was a terrible driver.

One of the most challenging and interesting cases I had in La Feria was an unconscious five-year-old boy who was thrust into my examining room in a state of shock, barely breathing and foaming at the mouth. We started artificial respiration while I was looking for clues and a diagnosis. When I asked the family what happened, they said he was drowned. I asked "Where was he drowned? In the front yard" was the reply. " Do you have a swimming pool there?" "No!" was the surprising reply. This whole episode wasn't making sense, and I pressed on with my exam and encountered not only excessive salivation, confused with drowning, but pinpoint pupils, which suggested organophosphate poisoning. Those chemicals were used in the early days of Valley farming. We started the antidote, intravenous atropine, and he began to regain consciousness. Fortunately the little fellow survived this near death experience.

Not so for one farm worker in Los Fresnos, who suffered from ticks and decided he would get rid of them quickly by applying concentrated methyl-parathion to his affected skin. He was dead within an hour.

One morning soon thereafter, I walked into the emergency room at Valley Baptist to find some thirty-five farm workers who entered a cotton field to hoe weeds that had been sprayed with methyl-parathion the night before. A heavy dew the next morning dissolved the residual methyl-parathion and quickly penetrated the dew soaked pants of the farm workers. Their skin absorbed the poison rapidly. They were retching, vomiting and in various states of sub-lethal poisoning. Fortunately all survived. Organophosphates are improved and much better controlled today. The agricultural community is gaining a high level of awareness about the handling of all types of pesticides.

One of the greatest friendships I made in the La Feria area was with a grumpy old farmer of Belgian extraction by the name of Howard Lievens. We put up with each other's onerousness well enough to become best friends over many years. I was fascinated by his skills on the farm. He grew row crops such as corn, grain and cotton, as well as developing wonderful citrus acreage featuring the latest cultures of pink and red grapefruit, as well as navel oranges. He was an innovative mechanic who kept a fully equipped shop in his barn and could build or repair almost

90

anything he needed in farm equipment. I loved to spend time with him.

One of his best clients was a New Haven Neurosurgeon, Lycurgis Davy, whose Wall Street advisor told him to invest in citrus in the Rio Grande Valley of Texas! He did and Howard became his grove care manager. He bought land and planted citrus on the periphery of Brownsville and Harlingen, after carefully studying the growth patterns of these cities. His wife, Artemis, loved to come to the Valley with him and became very attached to the Lievens family. They savored many happy Winter days enjoying the balmy weather of South Texas when their home state of Connecticut was frozen over.

Howard fashioned a hedger and topper machine that pruned his citrus trees and kept them from becoming too tall, and the hedger maintained the space between rows. Trimming the outer branches also encouraged inside growth where premium large fruit developed. That was money in the bank for the gift fruit shippers who valued large grapefruit.

I was very busy in my practice and Sarah, of course, was busy at home. I guess I was beginning to wonder if I was doing the right thing for my family. We had good help at home and good help at the office. The community was friendly and we were happy at St. Francis Xavier Parish just half a block from home. The older children seemed happy in school at St. Anthony's in Harlingen. Sarah became active in the children's school activities as a volunteer in their various projects. Life was good, but I often thought about the classmates that I knew well and I wondered how they were doing in their various professional pursuits. I talked a somewhat reluctant wife into a three-week vacation wherein we would travel leisurely about the country and visit some of my classmates and compare our lives with theirs. We arranged for Jackie Eddleblute and her husband Dana to be surrogate parents in our absence, along with two young, but quite mature, high school girls that we knew well.

Our first stop was Austin, where we found Grover Bynum, and his lovely wife Anita Schneider, a young Minnesota farm girl from Westbrook. Grover was enjoying life as a young Mayo-trained internist in a very prestigious group of men with similar backgrounds. Anita was very friendly, and we immediately knew we would always have a bed and breakfast in Austin. We still visit each other's homes and share life's ups and downs as true friends do. I knew I was not equipped to do what he was doing and we moved on to Benton, Arkansas to check on Rex and Tee.

They had started their family shortly after we did. They had previously moved to Florida, where Rex worked for the prison system a short time before he took a residency in Pediatrics and was boarded in that specialty. He had returned to Arkansas and his beloved Razorbacks and was working for Alcoa Metals in Benton. His home was filled with Razorback memorabilia and background music featuring the Razorback fight song and Alma Mater. For years, our group reunited for the annual battle between Arkansas and Texas.

Then our vacation travels led us to Fayetteville and the home of Bud and Lil Patrick where he was in family practice and doing very well. I was amazed at the scope of his practice and the skills he had developed. He had become a very fine family doctor after his residency at Pineville. It was Fall and the weather had turned cold, and I remember Lil tucking us in bed with heavy quilts to keep us warm, a problem we didn't have in the Rio Grande Valley.

Our last visit would be with two classmates in Neosho, Missouri, Paul Anderson and George Olive. Paul's dad was Superintendent of Schools there and his sister Phyllis married our classmate George Olive who was from Alabama, similar to my sister marrying Jim McCutchon. They talked George into moving to Neosho, where they practiced in a multidisciplinary clinic as family doctors. Paul wanted us to join them, and I promised to think about it. Having worked at the Kingsville Clinic, I had a preview of what that would be like and I was not sure I would have the autonomy I wanted.

On the way home we stopped by the University of Texas-School of Medicine in Galveston to visit Dr. Truman Blocker, Chairman of the Department of Surgery, to investigate the possibility of a residency in plastic and reconstructive surgery, should I decide to specialize. Dr. Blocker visited with me while he was attending his residents, many of whom were having considerable difficulty communicating with a Hispanic, non-English speaking male. I translated for them and Dr. Blocker was impressed. I believe I could have had the residency position right then and there if I had wanted it. However, after serious thought it didn't take me long to realize that I didn't have the artistic talent nor the imagination to be a really fine plastic surgeon. I realized that I was right where the Good Lord wanted me to be. My mind was clear and I was energized feeling that Sarah and I were where we were supposed to be. When we arrived home, our kids were overjoyed, appreciative of our worth, and made us promise never to leave them that long again.

By this time we were expecting our seventh child. Our parents were "freaking out", to put it in the vernacular. I don't know if we just never mastered the "Rhythm System", or if our connubial urges overcame our rational behavior. I do know that we were a very happy family and enjoying caring for our growing progeny.

Then we hit a couple of snags. Sarah came down with an atypical pneumonia and was admitted to the hospital. I had just made a house call at the farm home of Howard Lievens on North Kansas City Road and was returning to old Highway 83 to go to Valley Baptist Hospital and check on Sarah. Just as I approached the railroad tracks, in my preoccupied state of mind, I heard a train whistle that sounded as if it was in the front seat with me! I looked toward Harlingen and saw nothing, then looked to the right and there she was!   Bearing down on me at 30 mph and only about 60 yards away! I jammed on the breaks, and sure enough I killed the engine "smack dab" in the middle of the tracks. I turned the key to start the engine, but it didn't respond because the gear wasn't in neutral or park position. I felt that this was not a very intelligent way to die and the clock was ticking and the train whistle was working overtime at a deafening range. I threw open the car door for a dramatic leap and felt the restraint of my safety belt holding me securely in the driver's seat. With one rapid sweeping motion of my hand (faster than Wyatt Earp), I released the belt, jumped from the car, took about three giant steps, and when I looked over my right shoulder my car was flying through the air about 15 feet above the ground.

The train ground to a laborious halt, a crowd gathered and the engineer gave me a lecture on driving safety and pointed out a small dent in the cow catcher for which I would be billed by the train company. Oddly enough, I was given a ride home by my friend and patient, Fergus Reynolds, a local aviator and crop duster pilot, who's workaday life consisted of hours of boredom interrupted by moments of sheer terror. He, of all people, could identify with my near death experience. Fergus has passed on, but I continued caring for his mother, his wife and two of his brothers.

Fergus dropped me off at home and I hugged the children and realized how much I loved them. I headed for the hospital to apprise Sarah of my good fortune before someone else scared her with the story. I repeated the hugs and kisses and thanksgiving to the Lord for saving me so that I could continue to care for my family and my patients. The only residual of the accident is a gut-wrenching Pavlovian reflex every time I hear a train whistle.

Sarah recovered from her atypical pneumonia and Frank Allen Ferris was born on May 16, 1962. His name honored his Allen ancestors, and they all came to see the little fellow and admired his fair and blonde features, which differed from the olive complexions and brunette features of our Lebanese heritage.

One cannot deny the human trait of prejudice that permeates various societies the world over. Ethnic and religious wars and persecutions have existed throughout history. My Benedictine education in high school and the good nuns of Incarnate Word purged most of those primal instincts from my being. What they missed, our Negro maid took care of when I used the 'N' on her in one of my rebellious moments. She gave me a real bottom-blistering whipping that ended any trace of prejudice left in my body and soul. I'll forever thank her for that bit of insight into human dignity.

Now back to the memorable emergencies of a general practitioner who never suffered boredom. As mentioned before, La Feria was a real farming community. Though these families lived outside of town, they were considered to be La Ferian's. The La Feria Co-Op Gin was their meeting place for coffee, gossip and farm news of the day. They were the Bauers, the Phillipps, the Lievens, the Wolfs, Tom Caruso, and the gin manager, Dan Robinson. There were more but I couldn't keep up with all of them.

It was a little after midnight one quiet evening, and I was sound asleep until rudely awakened by one of the Bauer boys saying, "Come quick, Doc! Carl Bauer is in the drain ditch with a big tractor on top of him!" Good Lord, I thought! Please help me help him. I grabbed a pair of pants and my doctor bag and headed south to the Bauer farm where I found a frightening scene. Carl was on his back in about one foot of water, pinned under a giant, upside down tractor. One fellow was holding his head out of the water so he could breathe. I was able to give him some IV morphine to alleviate his pain and was in the process of starting IV fluid when one of the local farmers arrived with a house jack. The men were able to jack up the tractor so they could pull Carl out and get him in an ambulance and on his way to the hospital. Bob Jackson, a thoracic surgeon, met us in the emergency room and we took him straight to the operating room and labored through the night putting him back together. In those days, I did a lot of assisting in surgery, and I really enjoyed it. Carl's diaphragm was ruptured and his left lung was completely collapsed due to his intestines filling his entire left chest cavity. Dr. Jackson finished rearranging Carl's organs into their normal position, and the Old Dutchman survived this ordeal. I believe forever after he slowed down a bit turning on those canal corners and worked mostly in daylight hours

It wasn't too long after this that Sarah's namesake joined the family circle. Sarah Jane Ferris (the 2nd) was born at Valley Baptist on December 16, 1963, and what a beautiful child she was. We couldn't have asked for a better Christmas gift than this dear child. She was our largest infant weighing a bit over 9 pounds at birth. Now we had 4 girls and 4 boys and everything was even again. Life went well until Labor Day when we had our annual Harlingen Country Club Member-Guest Golf Tournament.

We invited the Bynum's from Austin and the Bailey's from Houston and told them to bring their kids. We would rent a condo on the South Padre Island, and the guys would play golf and the wives and kids would romp on the beach and in the surf. We did have a grand time and Johnny Bailey played Jim Cason a finals match for the championship that was packed with excitement. Jim Cason barely won in extra holes and we were so proud of Johnny Bailey's performance. There was cause for great celebration over Johnny's golfing skills. Everyone returned to our respective homes very happy because of the wonderful reunion.

The following Thursday I was still pumped up and went out to see if my game continued to improve. Then I received a very disturbing phone call indicating that Sarah was at the Valley Baptist Emergency Room with Sarita because the baby was very ill. I raced to the hospital where I found our Pediatrician, George

Willeford, attending Sarita with Sarah at the bedside. A spinal tap had already been done establishing a diagnosis of meningococcal meningitis, a highly contagious disease. This serious infectious disorder is especially prone to occur at get-togethers where diverse groups assemble for the first time. Some of these guests will be non-ill carriers of meningococcal disease and others will never have had any exposure and be extremely vulnerable to acquire the infection. Gatherings in Army recruiting centers and college campuses with incoming freshmen are particular hotbeds of this exposure. Fortunately, we now have a vaccine for meningococcal disease and our young people are encouraged to be immunized.

Sarah deserves the major portion of credit for saving Sarita's life. She took one quick look at the child and saw the sudden onset of pallor and lethargy and knew instinctively that something was terribly wrong. She was going into septic shock and near death. Sarah swept Sarita up in her arms, jumped in the car and headed straight for Dr. Willeford's office. He astutely recognized the problem, sent them to the hospital ER, did the spinal tap, and started IV antibiotics. Sarita remained comatose for three days. We will always be grateful to Dr. John Welty, Dr. Willeford's partner, who stayed at Sarita's bedside all the first night of her hospitalization to be sure her airway and blood pressure remained stable and her fluid requirements were met with appropriate IV solutions. There were no intensive care units in those days and the selfless dedication of doctors like Willeford and Welty often meant the difference between life and death. Today Sarita is happily married to a good husband, Curtis Koop from Edna, Texas, and the mother of three fine boys, Jack, Jeffrey, and Jake. Curtis and Sarita are both Aggies who met at the Dixie Chicken in College Station and now reside in Sugarland, Texas, where Sarita is an elementary school teacher and Curtis works in the food industry. We love to visit them. Jack is studying construction science at Texas A&M, and Jeffrey and Jake are still at home. We will see them this coming weekend on our way to New Orleans and my

60th medical class reunion.

The community of La Feria was very good to us, and we made many close friends there. Besides our friends in agriculture, there were Gilbert & Jackie Neese, who owned and operated Neese Pharmacy; Jay Hawkins, who was in the insurance business and his dear wife Priscilla, a school teacher; Moore and Glenda Matthews, who are still very close to us unto this day, had the State Farm Insurance Agency. The Matthews now live in Three Rivers and still come to see me for advice on medical issues.

Jay sold his 300 Savage deer rifle to Sarah to present to me as a Christmas gift and then invited me to go to his deer lease. He put me in a blind on a sendero and a buck deer stuck his head, front legs and big rack out of the brush less than 5 yards from my position! I was flabbergasted and squeezed off the closest shot I would ever have as a deer hunter. Nothing happened except a "click" of the trigger because I had failed to completely close the shell chamber. I made too many metallic sounds trying to get the shell chamber closed, and the deer wised up and my last sight of him was a white tail wagging at me as he disappeared in the brush on the other side of the sendero.

One of the joys of life in the Rio Grande Valley is the acculturation of two peoples, divided by the Rio Grande River, whose humanity becomes so obvious as they adapt to the vagaries of their diverse family and language backgrounds. This philosophical musing entered my thought process as I felt the need to define the word "*sendero*", which my computer rejected as unknown to its English vocabulary. After fifty-five years of life in the Rio Grande Valley, I often find myself mixing the two languages in my conversation with Hispanic people, but never outside of the areas of medicine and farming. I am far from being truly bilingual. I regret not pursuing the study of the Spanish language to its perfection. I have a similar regret regarding Arabic. Life is short and time is precious. I confess to having wasted many precious hours.

November 17, 1965, brought another angel into our family in the person of Jeanne Louise Ferris, named in honor of my wonderful sister, Jeanne Ferris McCutchon. Her husband and my classmate, Jim, has been my soul mate for all these years and I call him 'Bro' in the truest sense of the word. I could not love a brother any more than I love this stalwart man who remained at my sister's side to the very end. They lost two of their sons from the complications of heritable mental illness, and Jim supports another daughter who has been wise enough, at times, to accept medication. My attempts to help have fallen short of my goals although I still communicate with her about family. She possesses the beautiful name of Claire Amalie Clotilde McCutchon and she is a dear soul.

Now I'll go back to our beautiful newborn baby girl Jeanne. Our family welcomed child number nine with much pomp and circumstance. After all, we were now one ahead of the McCutchon's! Sarah seemed so happy with her contributions in time and effort for the good of St. Anthony's school. Each of our children would remain there through the eighth grade and plan to finish in the public schools of La Feria.

Other forces began to evolve that would dramatically change our lives. An outstanding group of Internal Medicine specialists in Harlingen began operating under the name of Valley Diagnostic Clinic. The members were all very bright and practiced very high quality medicine. They had watched my work for years and were impressed enough to ask me to consider going back to a residency in Internal Medicine for three years and then coming back to practice with them. I was honored, but the thought of going back on a resident's salary with nine children to feed and a wife about to lose the support of her household helpers was too much to bear. Also I considered the study and on-call duty would keep me away from the family most of the time. Then they suggested going back for one year and accepting the fact I would never be Board Certified. Even that was too much. I didn't want to completely abandon the opportunity so I offered a plan I could live with. At that time, Harvard Medical School offered an intensive review of the entire field of Internal Medicine. The course lasted for one month and was taught by the actual professors who were considered experts in their respective fields. Classes started at 8 a.m. and ended at 5 p.m. three days a week, and we went until 8 p.m. on Tuesdays and Thursdays, and for 4 hours on Saturday mornings. They could bring us up to date on the field of Internal Medicine with 192 hours of lectures in the space of four weeks. I would complete that intense course and then come home and make early morning rounds on our hospital patients with Dr. Garner Klein for a period of one year. He was a great teacher and the best clinician I have ever known. Although he cared most about the field of Cardiology, he knew the broad field of Internal Medicine very well. He was quiet, reflective and kind to his patients and his peers although stressed by the latter quite often. More than any one I have ever known, he exhibited the quality of equanimity, a virtue Sir William Osler said was a physician's most precious asset. Dr. Klein had the ability to remain calm and in control no matter what events occurred around him. He was a great teacher for me. Today I am honored to be his primary doctor, and he calls upon me when he is challenged medically. He and his wife, Nancy, operate a small beef farm that features a Brahman/Angus cross yielding a high quality of certified grass-fed beef marketed locally on a small scale.

On January 1, 1969, I left La Feria with some sadness in my heart and became an employee of the Valley Diagnostic Clinic, with full partnership in two years if the arrangement was successful. A new era had begun, and Sarah and I felt we were doing the right thing for our family's future. I would concentrate on adult and geriatric medicine, and forego Obstetrics, Pediatrics and any major surgery or assisting in surgery.

My trip to Boston would take place in April of 1969. I had the good fortune of a great friendship with a very successful pharmacist, R. A. Murphy, Jr., and his lovely and talented wife, Lynn. Bob, as everyone knew him, operated MacPherson's Pharmacy and bought out the legendary pharmacist, Ken MacPherson, to become the sole owner.

Bob's dad was known as The Tenor of Boston, and he passed that gift of song to his son, who was a great vocalist in his own right. Bob and Lynn gifted Harlingen with an era of the greatest duo in music and song imaginable. They did musicals, weddings, funerals, special events, operettas, and fund raisers selflessly. They provided the music for all five of our daughter's weddings.

To get back to the matter of the Harvard post-graduate course, Bob insisted that his dad should meet my plane and take me to their home for a couple of nights until I could find lodging for the month. Bob Senior and Doris were two of the happiest and nicest persons I had ever met. They lived in Arlington, a suburb of Boston, and they counseled me on how to ride the bus to Harvard Square, from where I would catch the subway downtown, and transfer to another subway that would drop me right by the Medical School. My transportation was solved.

About the second day of school and successful travel, I arrived rather late one evening and Bob and Doris proposed that after some discussion they felt I should turn off my search for a suitable abode and just stay with them.

One evening when I arrived from school, Doris said, "The Cardinal called and wants you to join him for lunch at his residence". I was surprised and delighted about the invitation. I had known Cardinal Medeiros when he was Bishop of the Diocese of Brownsville, which included Harlingen and La Feria. He was a gentle and saintly man who bore no pretense of royalty as evidenced by his invitation to this small town physician. Perhaps he had been pleased by my efforts to make emergency medical care more available to indigent families whose children were dying from diarrhea and dehydration because of lack of financial resources.

A group of nuns headed by Sister Marian Strohmeyer reached out to help families understand the dangers of infant diarrheas and the accompanying dehydration that could quickly take their little lives. Often the excuse for delayed diagnosis and treatment was lack of money to enter the private medical delivery system. The Medicaid program did not exist at that time. I felt we needed a group of doctors willing to volunteer to run a small evening clinic and see ill children before the little tykes were in grave danger. I was able to recruit 13 additional volunteer physicians who would take one night of duty every two weeks. The Sisters named their effort Su Clinica Familiar.

Bob Murphy had a very small office behind MacPherson's Pharmacy and donated enough space for the little clinic to open. We operated quite successfully for a few months, and I think we made a slight impact but realized there was much more to be done. Since many of our patients were migrant workers, we thought about trying to get some funds through the Migrant Health program. If I had it to do over, I would have put more effort into pursuing private philanthropic sources, but I was not good about asking people for money and I really didn't understand anything about raising private funds. I was naive enough to underestimate the future implications of accepting Federal money and the inevitable bureaucratic control by people who really did not know our area and its problems. Nevertheless, I continued to travel to Washington D. C., on an annual basis to secure more funds and be sure we were in compliance with Federal regulations. We actually were able to hire a full-time physician by this time. Dr. Bill Heusel and his wife Mona brought their children from Nebraska and answered this call to a missionary-like situation. The Diocese of Brownsville was the local shepherd of these Migrant funds and my role lessened. A governing board consisting of local citizens and health care professionals gave direction to the effort. Today Su Clinica is a giant Federal entity containing dozens of examining rooms and a large paid staff. The last two patients I referred there with sub-acute problems were unable to be seen for two months. Such is the efficiency so characteristic of government medicine. "Too soon old; too late wise!"

Armed with the knowledge of Internal Medicine that I learned at the Harvard review course, I settled in with my four internist associates and began early morning rounds with Dr. Klein. The literature now showed that patients with acute heart attacks should be cared for in a specialized setting to be called coronary care units or CCU's. These units featured specially trained people who could respond quickly to cardiac emergencies. It also includes all the necessary equipment for resuscitation and defibrillation. Generous supplies of all emergency drugs were also present in handy portals. Respiratory equipment was available for persons needing respiratory assistance. We were trained, practiced and ready to go. This environment was a far cry from the emergency thoracotomy adventure I experienced in the Philippines.

All of the Valley Diagnostic Clinic doctors met every morning at 7 a.m. to read EKG's and talk about any problem patients. Then Dr. Klein and I would trot off to round on our own patients, and these rounds were invaluable teaching moments from Dr. Klein's vast knowledge of Internal Medicine. After a year with him and my experience at the intense post-graduate course at Harvard, I felt comfortable in the practice of Internal Medicine although I could never be board certified nor could I be considered thoroughly trained in a formal program. I believe some of my family doctor colleagues criticized my decision to follow this path and practice with internists. I justified it as the best way to take care of my large family and learn more about Internal Medicine. I have never regretted that decision.

With nine children, we had certainly outgrown our little home in La Feria, and now my office was in Harlingen, and so we began to look at possibilities there. For several years, we had been members of the Harlingen Country Club whose members used the Tony Butler Municipal Golf Course for its golfing members. We enjoyed the venue, but when the Harlingen Clubhouse burned and the Harlingen Air Force Base closed, our small airport known as Harvey Richards Field, served by Trans-Texas Airways, moved on to bigger things. The Air Force Base field became the Harlingen International Airport, which preceded Valley International Airport after the arrival of Southwest Airlines, a commuter airline linking Houston, San Antonio, and Dallas.

Herb Kelleher, a Southwest Airlines founder and friend of David Allex, local Executive Director of the Harlingen Chamber of Commerce, put Harlingen on the map when David prevailed on Herb to make Harlingen the fourth site for Southwest. The entire Rio Grande Valley was covered by Southwest because of Harlingen's strategic central location. This was a brilliant move by both men and certainly a great boon to Harlingen's future.

A coalition of Harlingen Country Club leaders such as Hill Cocke, Van Snell, Al Jones, Bert Keys and others envisioned the old airport as a site for a new Harlingen Country Club and 18 hole golf course surrounded by an upscale residential subdivision to include large lots with big homes, condos, and smaller haciendas segregated to maintain values for the different types of adjoining structures. These leaders formed an entity known as the Harlingen Development Corporation, which purchased the old airport and then sold sufficient land to the Harlingen Country Club for a golf course, clubhouse, swimming pool, tennis courts, maintenance, and cart storage barns. The remaining portion of the land was used for various classes of homes to suit a wide variety of individual needs. An independent township was established with its own city government separate and apart from the city of Harlingen. The township was named Palm Valley. It had its own city government, police department, sewage plant, contract for electrical services, taxing body for revenue and became a separate entity. Lots were put on the market for sale and Caro Circle was the first Cul-de-sac to be developed. Straws were drawn to determine which buyer would have first choice. I think Sarah and I were in 3rd place, and we chose Lot #8 on Caro Circle, which was a beautiful venue backing up to the 17th fairway about 50 to 75 yards in front of the 17th green. We observed and I participated in many memorable golfing moments in that short stretch of real estate. How we've loved living there! The kids had acres of ground on which to run and play as we were only the second home to be built in Palm Valley.

Grover and Anita Bynum suggested we consult an architect friend of theirs by the name of Frank Whitson. We loved working with Frank and getting to know his wife Midge. Frank designed a beautiful two-story home for us that featured tall glass panels rising around a very large front door. The floor plan was spacious around the entry and reminded us of homes we had seen in the movies. I was so excited I hustled over to my builder Dana Eddleblute's home and presented him with the plan. "What do you think?" Dana just laughed and retorted, you couldn't begin to afford this home! Go back and tell him to build it like a box!" We did just that! It came back as a 60' x 40' rectangle with decorative curving brick walls that made a small patio outside the master bedroom and another curved wall with an iron gate leading to the kitchen. It was a functionally superb plan for a large family. The front entrance was recessed under an overhanging bedroom to further break up the box look. A separate three-car garage with large storage closets connected with the kitchen patio. Upstairs, six monastery-like bedrooms faced south with only a bed, closet and study desk for six of our children who wanted a private bedroom. These rooms had removable walls so that six bedrooms could eventually become three after the children left home. Our two youngest daughters preferred a larger bedroom together. Our two oldest took slightly larger bedrooms across the hall from the dormitory rooms. Our baby boy, David, born five years after the others, didn't need a bedroom until Kaki left for college. Problem solved!

The crowning glory of our home was a double fireplace that was constructed entirely of petrified wood estimated to be 20 million years old. These stones were hand gathered by Sarah, myself, and the donors, Doris and Chick Powers who lived on a ranch very near Tilden, Texas. Howard Lievens and I brought two pickup loads of the petrified wood home and the Mexican artisans who built our home fashioned them into the floor-to-ceiling structure that separates our family room from our living room. It is a rare treasure that can no longer be bought or sold.

Meanwhile, the kids were thriving in school and at home where the older boys, John III and Chris, enjoyed jumping in the golf course water holes and finding balls and turtles. Since we were the second home to be built in Palm Valley, there was lots of open space for them to run and play. Our builder was Tilton Garrison from San Benito, a congenial and lovable soul who worked with a crew from Mexico. These artisans loved their calling and worked so well with Tilton. They were a crew of four and they could do everything the architect planned including the design and construction of the petrified wood fireplace. The story is chronicled in a photographic album from foundation to finish. The home has been through four hurricanes and "never shivered a timber"! We are so blessed to have lived in this home for forty-four years, but alas, we're in the age of small families and now that we're ready to find a much smaller place there don't seem to be any large families. Such is life!

The heart of this home is a valiant woman whose early life began in Corpus Christi, on May 20, 1930. I have written before of her heritage but now I want to write of her life as a Wife and Mother. I have capitalized those terms because she has fulfilled those roles with honor. There is no better description of her life than one finds in Proverbs, Chapter 31, Verses 10-31. I am compelled to quote these verses in an older translation because it better suits the romantic emotions we experienced as young lovers.

"Who shall find a valiant woman? far and from the uttermost coasts is the price of her.

The heart of her husband trusteth in her, and he shall have no need of spoils.

She will render him good, and not evil, all the days of her life.

She hath sought wool and flax, and hath wrought by the counsel of her hands.

She is like the merchant's ship, she bringeth her bread from afar.

And she hath risen in the night, and given a prey to her household, and victuals to her maidens.

She hath considered a field, and bought it: with the fruit of her hands she hath planted a vineyard.

She hath girded her loins with strength, and hath strengthened her arm.

She hath tasted and seen that her traffic is good: her lamp shall not be put out in the night.

She hath put out her hand to strong things, and her fingers have taken hold of the spindle.

She hath opened her hand to the needy, and stretched out her hands to the poor.

She shall not fear for her house in the cold of snow: for all her domestics are clothed with double garments.

She hath made for herself clothing of tapestry: fine linen, and purple is her covering.

Her husband is honourable in the gates, when he sitteth among the senators of the land.

She made fine linen and sold it, and delivered a girdle to the Chanaanite.

Strength and beauty are her clothing, and she shall laugh in the latter day.

She hath opened her mouth to wisdom, and the law of clemency is on her tongue.

She hath looked well to the paths of her house, and hath not eaten her bread idle.

Her children rose up and called her blessed: her husband, and he praised her.

Many daughters have gathered together riches: thou hast surpassed them all.

Favour is deceitful, and beauty is vain: the woman that feareth the Lord, she shall be praised.

Give her of the fruit of her hands: and let her works praise her in the gates."

Our children, grandchildren, and now great grandchildren, have been so blessed to have this living, loving Wife and Mother in our lives. What a gift!

Sometime before this, while I was still in La Feria and before Expressway 83 was open, I would travel to Valley Baptist Hospital by turning south on the old Brownsville Highway and then cut east to the hospital on a gravel road known as Ed Carey. It was a straight and easy shot to my destination. There was only one undeveloped cross road, Hale, and a railroad track before hitting Sunshine Strip and the Valley Baptist neighborhood. I visualized this gravel road as a major thoroughfare in the future and I was "dead on"!

While still in La Feria, I had made friendships with Drs. Tom Klug, Fred Muniz and John Tucker. One of my dreams was a multidisciplinary partnership of compatible doctors to form a group practice. Tom, as a general surgeon, needed to keep his referral base as broad as possible so he wasn't interested in such a plan. John Tucker joined a group practice in San Benito. I encouraged Tom and Fred to meet with Bob Scoggins and me to consider trying to form an investment group to purchase this 18 acre strip of land that fronted Ed Carey - from the Old Brownsville Highway all the way to Hale - a distance greater than the length of 6 football fields. The average depth was greater than 300 feet, so it was perfectly suited for commercial frontage development. We notified the realtor representing the owners, who were in Houston, and for three months the realtor did nothing. One rainy Thursday afternoon when I was free from my appointment schedule, I went by Bob's office to vent my frustrations with their realtor, and we decided to call the owners directly. They were informed that we were interested, and after consideration for a few days, they were willing to sell for a price of $1550 an acre or $27,900. This was a fair price for good irrigated farmland in the Rio Grande Valley. We talked to Nathan Winters, President of San Benito Bank & Trust, and he loaned us the money. The Robert M. Scoggins Trust was born with the help of Martin Ferrero, our attorney. We were off to a long and exciting future as an investment trust with one surgeon to cut our expenses; two medical doctors to treat our headaches and ulcers, and a CPA, to protect us from the IRS.

After about six months, we sent Tom and Bob to San Antonio to talk to Conoco about purchasing our highway corner as a future service station site. They came back with a check to the Trust for $40,000 for a 200' site. We paid the bank and began to think of what to do next? My experience in observing my farmer friends made me suggest that we put the land to work as a vegetable farm as the acreage was too small to make any money farming row crops such as cotton, grain or corn. We were aware that many Valley farmers of Japanese heritage were excellent vegetable growers. We approached Mutsu Kawamura and arranged for him to share in the profits, but be protected from any expenses or losses, and he liked the agreement and planted 16 acres of lettuce along our Ed Carey frontage. Fortunately we hit a great lettuce market and banked another $6,000, or $333 net profit per acre. The next lettuce season we tripled the size of our lettuce crop by renting additional land and had to plow it under because there was no market. That was the last lettuce adventure for the Scoggins Trust. We would devote our attention to other investments. Shortly thereafter, we purchased 5 acres on the opposite corner of Ed Carey and Hale Avenue to hold for the future. We felt we were doing well in real estate and would keep an eye out for additional opportunities. We held periodic meetings for lunch at the Oyster Bar and really enjoyed discussing our ventures.

My medical priorities never took a back seat to my interest in business, farming or investments. The opposite neglect was true. At one time my broker, Monte Custer with Merrill Lynch in Corpus Christi, tried desperately to get in touch with me because a futures position I held in wheat was unexpectedly crumbling rapidly. In fact, during the previous hour, I had lost $20,000. At one time I was told by Monte that I was ranked as Merrill Lynch's most profitable single commodity trader in the United States; a dubious honor that ended with my wheat debacle.

Actually, I am a risk taker whose irrational motive was to support my family through investment, and not through the practice of medicine. I never wanted any of my practice decisions to depend on the patient's ability to pay. I think I have adhered to that philosophy. The problem is that I was trained to be a physician and I'm good at medicine. I've had no formal training in business, and I am not good at management, but it hasn't stopped me from trying. I do have good judgment in matters of raw land potential and the management and development of that type of real estate.

Under the leadership of my son Frank (Pancho), a very bright Civil Engineer, we have developed two upscale residential subdivisions known as Nueces Park and Avalon, both of which rest on land that I purchased and farmed. We have been through seven years of a depressed economy and 'holding on' has been really tough, but we are beginning to see the light. I planted pecan trees on the frontage of Nueces Park with plans to reserve that ground for commercial development. A poorly informed and incompetent realtor told a client that the frontage would always be a pecan grove. When we started commercial development of the frontage, hysteria broke out in the subdivision among a small group of residents, and they met with a pro bono attorney and sued us to block that development. Two of those litigants were my colleagues. I couldn't believe it! Initially they included the owner of the real estate firm but soon exempted her from the suit. Sarah and I were left with $70,000 in legal and insurance expenses and a great deal of heartache. We recently sold this subdivision to one of the finest and truest friends I've ever had. Matt and Patty Gorges knew of our plight and came to the rescue and they, with their son Michael, are keeping our cash flow going for a while. Their office is in Pecan Plaza, and I know they will see this project to its ultimate conclusion.

Over the next few years, The Robert M. Scoggins Trust met regularly and increased its activity to include the purchase of the old Judy Lin Motel on the corner of Ed Carey and Sunshine Strip. We eventually demolished the property and replaced it with sales to McDonald's, an active convenience store, an auto repair garage, a Taco Bell and the Trust became financially more solid.

I had spotted two more tracts of land that I thought had growth potential for the Trust. One was on the freeway at the southeast corner of Helen Moore where a 5-acre tract of highway frontage was undeveloped. The other was a 200-acre tract of farmland on the highway to Rio Hondo, with extended highway frontage on the north and backing up to significant Arroyo Colorado waterfront on the south. Considering that this property was primarily farmland, we needed a real farmer in our group. I immediately thought of my grumpy, but wise and highly capable friend from La Feria, Howard Lievens. The group approved the nomination and Howard accepted and became an equal partner in a new entity known as the F & S Trust. This Trust was the old group of Scoggins, Muniz, Klug and Ferris that now included Howard Lievens with expertise in agriculture.

We arranged for our 200-acre purchase to be farmed by a renter, sold construction sand from the banks of the Arroyo Colorado, and sold a portion of the land to a pajama manufacturer for their plant. All the Trust members were pleased.

The shrimp industry was a major contributor to the Valley's economy. Through our medical and surgical practices, Dr. Klug and I had become acquainted with Vivian and Buster Harris of Port Isabel. These transplants from Kentucky had come to the Rio Grande Valley to participate in the fishing industry, particularly shrimp fishing. Buster, like my friend Howard Lievens, was a multi-talented individual who said he could build us a fine shrimp boat if we were interested in investing in the fishing industry. We watched in amazement, from the laying of the keel to the launch, the construction of this beautiful 90 feet, all metal, freezer boat that we named *Ensolido*, to symbolize the steadfastness of our partnership and our trust in one another. We gathered our families and met for the maiden voyage of this beautiful vessel. How proud we were sailing out of the ship channel and into the Gulf of Mexico, four couples, 24 children, and a great boat builder who would manage our fishing enterprise. This venture was so successful we opted for a sister ship known as *Mas Solido*, to symbolize the increasing bond among the members of the Scoggins trust.

112

One smaller wooden iceboat was added to our fleet for nearby trips into the Gulf, but she could fish for only 4-5 days. One night when the crew was asleep, another boat collided with her and she sank with no injuries to the crew and everyone survived. Our insurance company paid for the loss of our vessel, but we received a lesson in the depth of our risk as participants in this industry.

As time marched on, I had been individually investing in all the land I could find across Stuart Place Road from the Harlingen Country Club. I felt the land had development potential, and until that happened, I had the help and advice of Papa Lievens to keep it under cultivation and financially productive. My sons, somewhat reluctantly at times, always had work to do at the farm caring for the pasture and the cattle we kept there. I think they learned a great deal about life, animals, crops and food production as well as land, investments, and a work ethic that is often the road to a secure future for one's family. They were actually willing workers, and I was proud of them and the lessons they learned about productivity and the real world.

Sarah was busy with the girls and their activities and as a real role model for who a mother should be. Swimming was the main athletic endeavor of our kids, and they were all involved. Tita excelled and was a member of a famous relay team that won many events for the Harlingen swim team. She later went to Lamar University on a swimming scholarship and completed two years there before transferring to the University of Texas. She lived at Newman Hall, on the same campus as Newman School where I attended first and third grade and learned to be an Altar Boy at St. Austin's Church. She went on to Texas A & M for graduate studies in Child Development and was being heavily courted by a young hospital administrator working at Valley Baptist by the name of Bill Adams. He made many a trip between Harlingen and College Station and convinced her that he was "The One". They live here now and have three wonderful children. Bill oversees two hospitals and provides love and care to his family and his in-laws.

Tita teaches kindergarten at Long Elementary and stays close to help take care of her Mom and Dad's needs. We're so proud of them. They gave us three wonderful grandchildren and a great grandson, Cory, from Billy and Kelly's marriage. Their second son, John Henry, married Carey Stevenson from San Antonio, a nurse who is just entering nurse practitioner school. John Henry is following in his dad's footsteps as a hospital administrator. Their daughter Amy Claire will graduate from Texas A & M with a degree in Animal Psychology and has spent her last two vacations working with dolphins. She's planning on continuing that work in the Dominican Republic after graduation. She is an adventuress and the only one in our family who has visited Australia and parachuted from a plane to Mother Earth. I wish she could meet President George H. W. Bush. He would love her spirit!

This is the perfect time to reintroduce my old roommate from Texas A & I, Charlie Winn. We lost touch with one another after I went to Tulane, and Charlie went to the University of Texas. As I mentioned before, we did accidentally run into one another at a dance in San Antonio and visited for just a few minutes. It was not until some 20 years later when we both had growing families that my stockbroker, Ben Hammond, remembered that I knew Charlie and sent me a newspaper clipping about Charlie helping out the finances in Maverick County by paying his taxes early. Charlie and Patsy had moved their family from San Antonio to their ranch near Eagle Pass where their family grew up, went to high school, married and began to raise their children. This was the kind of life the parents wisely chose to develop character, perseverance and a strong Christian faith in their children.

I sent Charlie a note about the newspaper article, and he responded by inviting me to come up and hunt with them at their lease on the Laureles division of the King Ranch. Access to their hunting lodge and guest cabins was the King ranch gate 2 miles south of Chapman Ranch, where they had leased some 35,000 acres. My father-in-law, Frank C. Allen, Jr., and I had often hunted geese in grain fields very close to Chapman Ranch headquarters, where the geese liked to feed. All that country was under dry land cultivation and home to crops such as cotton and grain sorghum. I never paid attention to the fact that 2 miles south began a ranch land of mesquite and laurel trees where some of the finest beef cattle in the world had been bred and born. The venue was a rolling landscape of brush, pastures and lakes that was home to the Santa Gertrudis breed of beef cattle. Deer, wild turkey, collared peccary (javelinas), coyotes, geese, sand hill cranes, roseate spoonbills, armadillos, roadrunners and rattlesnakes highlighted the local population of wildlife. It was a hunter's paradise.

Charlie and I renewed our friendship and began to know each other's families. Charlie had become very successful in the oil business. As a wildcatter, he had brought in a well near Pearsall, Texas, that set the record for the highest flow pressure ever recorded in the state of Texas - 19,000 barrels a day! Winn Exploration Company, with Charlie at the helm and his faithful assistant, Michael Cally, ever at his side, became a highly respected institution in the nation's oil and gas industry. Charlie was named Wildcatter of the Year in an exclusive national society limited by invitation only to the top 100 Wildcatters in the United States.

The trio of families that worked with their Dad and played major roles in the operation of Winn Exploration were Charlie and Nancy, Tom and Melissa, and Southern and Cathy. Charlie was an expert in finance and Tom and Southern were geologists. They were a close knit team involved in the family business while their wives made sure the home fronts were rich with Christian living and education. Grandmother Patsy was the true spiritual leader of the Winn clan and never let a day go by without her expression of love for Jesus Christ and thanksgiving for the many blessings bestowed on her family. She came from a large family in the Kerrville area that knew what it meant to be poor. As a young adult, she was working in a San Antonio office building where an aspiring young fellow in the oil business saw her stranded by a rain storm and offered her a ride home. The rest is the history related above.

Charlie and I felt good about the renewal of our relationship, and Sarah and I began to receive more invitations to visit the ranch. We met their children and grandchildren on these weekend trips and traveled with them to Santa Fe, New England in the Fall, and the commissioning of the George H. W. Bush aircraft carrier. We occasionally asked if we could bring friends that we wanted the Winn's to know. One memorable trip was with my dear friend and hunting companion, Howard Lievens. He was slowly dying of lung cancer. Charlie sent his pilot and private plane to pick up Howard and me and fly us to Corpus Christi and then drive to the Winn Lodge for an overnight sightseeing tour of the ranch and the game so plentiful on the ranch. Howard was thrilled and temporarily distracted from the battle he was fighting with his lung cancer. Shortly after that Howard had a heart attack in my car after one of his treatments at M.D. Anderson in Houston. I called the EMS to meet me at a certain intersection where I pulled Howard's body out of the car, laid him on the ground with the help of a passerby, and started resuscitation procedures. We were able to get his heart started again but never established real effective circulation, and he soon expired in the coronary care unit at Valley Baptist Hospital in Harlingen. His last words to me in the car, before he lost consciousness, were "Goodbye John", as I lost one of the best and truest friends I ever had. We loved to chide each other. When he and Betty visited us at home, I would place his chair under one of my big mounted deer heads to emphasize who was the better hunter and serve him a Manhattan cocktail to sooth his hurt feelings. We both loved the times we spent together. His son, Steve, who is every bit the man his father was, has always treated me with the greatest love and respect. Our feelings are mutual and there isn't anything I wouldn't do for that man and his wonderful wife Yoli. They are truly salt of the earth!

Dave Rogers, my Ag banker from Edinburg, and I joined Charlie for lunch at the lodge one day when Dave was in Corpus Christi for a bank meeting. Charlie and Dave later did a little business together.

Erin McCormick and her husband Mike Finger, both urologists, were special guests with Sarah and me for a weekend at the ranch. It was their first exposure to deer hunting in Texas, and I think they will always remember that trip.

Dr. Tom Klug and George McShan spent one weekend at the ranch with Charlie. They didn't hunt but were amazed at the bountiful wildlife. Tom has passed on since that visit, and I had the honor of caring for him until his last day on earth. He came in for a preventive health exam about two years before his death. I am a believer in routine chest x-rays as part of a periodic preventive health exam in my older population. Tom had a small nodule in his lung. He was so proud of me for finding such a small tumor and had the best surgeon he knew take it out. We all believed we had caught it in time. Unfortunately it recurred about one year later and eventually took his life. Three of the five members of the F & S Trust; Tom, Fred Muniz, and Howard all developed lung cancer and all three smoked, though Howard and Tom quit several years before developing the actual tumor. It makes my heart ache to be standing in line at the convenience store as young men and women buy pack after pack or cartons of cigarettes. I know so well what will happen to many of them as they later fight the addicting powerful nicotine. It's not only the cancer, for more commonly it is the ravages of cardiovascular disease that promotes the blockage of the arteries to the heart, brain and legs.

Two of the Winn's closest friends in Corpus Christi are Bert and Doris DuBois. They were nearly always visitors at the ranch when we were there. Bert is a retired insurance agent and keeps active raising beef cattle at Orange Grove, where he has a small pasture and some mother cows. Doris is a devoted wife and mother with boundless energy and conviviality to brighten anyone's day. She also can turn out the best chocolate pies in South Texas. Doris worked for Taylor Brother's Jewelers in Corpus Christi, when Charlie Winn came in as a customer to shop for a gift for his wife, Patsy. They learned from each other they had both lost daughters in the prime of their lives in untimely accidents. This common bond of heartache drew the Winn's and the DuBois' into a common understanding, sharing and caring that made their friendship grow and reach out to each other. They don't talk about it, but it is a bond of friendship that only those who suffered such loss can truly understand the heartache they endured.

The years from 1975 to 1995 were jam packed with action. We were in the prime of life and loving it. The medical practice was thriving and the children were active in school and swimming. It was a calm Sunday morning in 1976 when I received an unusual call from the Texas Department of Public Safety stating that one of my patients, an elderly lady, was in a hostage situation and having heart problems and wondered if I could be of help? I grabbed my emergency bag and headed for Motel 6 near the freeway where the gunman had holed up with his hostages, including the husband and daughter of my patient. As I approached the scene on the freeway, I noticed police snipers on the overpass, ready to "take out" the gunman if and when he decided to appear outside or move his location.

I found the police command post and was advised that the patient was lying on the floor with the gunman in control of a lobby including the other two family members and a DEA agent who had gone in unarmed to attempt to talk the gunman into surrendering. I don't remember anyone one else being involved.

This scenario really began much earlier in the day when this drug runner was identified as such and began a real war when he shot a border patrol officer at the Sarita checkpoint. He then fled in his car to Riviera, turned west to Premont, where he commandeered my patient, her husband and daughter and their vehicle at a service station. He then made a U-turn and headed back to Riviera, then turned South on US 77, with an entourage of various law enforcement vehicles trailing behind, but unable to act for fear of hurting one of the hostages. He drove until he reached the old Motel 6 in Harlingen, where he herded his hostages into the lobby where I suppose he intended to make a stand and/or bargain with the law.

When I entered the lobby, I observed my patient lying on the floor parallel to the front of a couch; the other two family members seated nearby and the DEA agent perched on the back of another sofa directly opposite and about 15 feet from the couch. The entire scene took place in a circular area no larger than 25 feet in diameter. The gunman was obviously quite nervous and continued to pace back and forth just a few feet at a time. My patient was trembling and had what I perceived to be a sinus tachycardia (rapid heart rate). I asked the gunman's permission to give her an IV tranquilizer to calm her fear and slow her heart rate. I had a little Valium in my bag and gave her only 2 mg. intravenously and almost immediately she relaxed and her heart rate slowed nicely to less than 100 beats per minute. She was able to get up and be comfortable in a chair.

Feeling that this was the opportune time to tell the gunman that I had noticed that he was quite tense and nervous, I offered to give him a small dose of IV Valium. He consented and I gave him just 5 mg slowly IV, and he quickly became quite calm. I told him that was all the Valium I had in my bag, but with his permission, I could return to the hospital and bring more because it appeared we might be in this situation for a long while. He consented and I left the scene and headed for the hospital where I loaded my syringe with 20 mg of Valium and returned to Motel 6. As I entered the front door, I took careful note of the fact that Louie, a respiratory therapist from the hospital, was there with his emergency breathing equipment.

The original Valium injection was still slightly effective so I stalled and waited until the gunman again appeared to be anxious. I asked if he thought he could use a little more Valium. He believed he could, but he wanted to rearrange the seating and warned me not to try anything funny. He brought the daughter to the couch to be on his left and positioned me to be in front and slightly to his right. He switched his pistol to his left hand and placed the tip of the barrel very close to her right temple.

I gained IV access to a good vein and ascertained that the needle was well placed in the vein and proceeded to inject the entire 20 mg of Valium as fast as I could. He did not detect that anything was different, and in about 12–15 seconds, he had a blank look on his face, his eyes crossed and the DEA agent leaped across my right shoulder and pinned the gunman's left arm against the wall, taking control of the pistol as it fell from his hand. Louie and the emergency crew rushed in and established an open airway and breathed for him as they rolled him to the waiting ambulance and headed to Valley Baptist Hospital.

In my earlier talks with the gunman I had promised him if he would surrender I would take him to the hospital and get him settled down before I would let the police take him to jail. About that time, a big tall Texas Ranger appeared and said, "We're taking him to jail." I said, "If you do, you'll do it against my orders." Our newly arrived hospital administrator, Ben McKibbens was observing this confrontation with great interest. Mr. McKibbens asked if I could assure him and the Ranger that this man wouldn't hurt any one before morning. I replied I could do that with appropriate sedation, and I would feel that I had not failed to keep my part of the negotiations for his surrender. I ordered sufficient sedation to keep him asleep until the Rangers arrived in the morning and transported him to Kingsville where he was jailed. The story had great reader appeal, and I think received worldwide publication. I know I received one letter from a friend who read it in a German newspaper and from many acquaintances in different parts of the United States.

A few days of notoriety went by, and I received a call from the Sheriff of Kleberg County stating that the prisoner wanted to see me. My good friend Pat Kornegay flew me to Kingsville in his private plane, and I visited with the jailed gunman. As I thought about my conversation with the prisoner, I didn't think there was much point to his request. I believe that he was trying to thank me for saving his life but just didn't know exactly how to put it into words. We shook hands, and Pat and I flew home making many low altitude circles over a hunting lease that Howard Lievens and I had just North of Raymondville. I had walked every foot of that ground with my son Paul, and we had one of our most memorable hunts there. I want to tell that story because it is the scenario of what real deer hunters are about.

It was late one afternoon, just before sunset when Paul and I found a fresh deer rub on the trunk of a small tree. Buck deer clean and sharpen their antlers by rubbing them on trees, which destroys the bark and leaves the raw wood exposed. This rub was very fresh. The bucks are very territorial and these rubs also mark what they believe to be the boundaries of their kingdom and the service of all the does therein. The bucks will cautiously return to this tree fairly often. Our hunting challenge was to be there when he returned. The first evening I went alone and climbed a tree about 35 yards downwind from the rub tree. The sun was setting when I heard the cautious and slow footsteps of an animal on the dry leaves directly behind me, probably about 20 yards away. I knew the buck was already suspicious because he was tiptoeing one step at a time. I was sure he had already detected my scent because he was downwind from my position in the tree. I dare not move or turn to look because he would immediately confirm his suspicions and take flight. Then all fell silent and I knew he was aware of my presence and had returned to a safer place. I waited a day and tried it again, but the buck didn't show up.

The pursuit of this wise old buck was becoming a real challenge. I knew it was going to require two hunters to bring him to the dinner table. I told Paul about the challenge, and we walked out one morning to develop a strategy. After surveying the situation, Paul suggested that he would climb a tree about 30 yards to the east-northeast of the rub tree, and I would be in a different tree than I had been in when the deer first spotted me, west-southwest of the rub tree.

We would be facing each other, but we would have every point on the compass covered. We knew each other's exact position so there was no danger of a shooting accident. We waited a couple of days and then took our respective positions about an hour and a half before sunset.

One of the beautiful attractions of hunting is the precious time that one has in the woods while waiting for something to happen. All sorts of thoughts and problems can become very clear in the silence of the wilderness. I treasured those moments in Mother Nature's arms and often thought my purpose in life became clearer and I became closer to my Creator.

Then, as if by magic, the buck appeared! Walking steadily toward his rub tree from the north-northwest, he was totally unaware of our presence, as there was no wind to carry our scent in his direction. "CRACK!" spoke Paul's rifle and the buck fell dead instantly.

I don't hunt deer any more. I've had all the thrills that sport offers and watching them brings back wonderful memories of good times with good people.

As we moved into the late 70's and in the 80's I became much more active in the governing bodies of the Valley Baptist Hospital, medical staff and the Valley Diagnostic Clinic. I was elected to serve as the Chief of the Medical Staff for two years. This job was thrust upon me by my colleagues, Drs. Tom Klug and Michael Fennegan as members of the nominating committee. Probably the crowning glory of my time there was to recognize the tremendous value of the contributions of Heinrich and Annie Lamm to the image of good medical care in the Rio Grande Valley. Heinrich and Annie and I became good friends as well as colleagues on the hospital staff. Our circle of close friends included Dr. Rudolph "Rudy" Hecht of La Feria, and his wife Ilse, who was a fast friend and moral supporter of Sarah. Ilse had studied nursing and excelled in that field of health care. The Hecht children, David, Tommy, Martin and Anita, were childhood friends of our children and some have stayed in contact to this day. After I moved to Harlingen, Rudy accepted a teaching job in family practice at the University of Wisconsin in Madison. The Hecht's occasionally returned to their condo on South Padre Island in the Summer, and we loved visiting them there but as we have all aged it has been more difficult to stay in touch.

I enjoyed the challenges of being Chief of Staff and the monitoring of administration and medical staff relationships and policies, but I cannot lay claim to any earthshaking accomplishments during my administration nor any catastrophes, thank goodness!

As we went into the late eighties, I was ready and desirous of taking over the helm of the Valley Diagnostic Clinic, and I actively campaigned for the position. I wanted VDC to continue to grow to its potential of being the shining light of Valley medicine. I realized the collective brainpower and skills of the likes of Howard Tewell, Garner Klein, Noel Searle, Bob Hatcher, John Reeder, Jocelyn Gonzalez, Darvey Fuller, Joe Dougherty and John Cooper in radiology. We were an effective team with a great laboratory and radiology service. I began to travel to major clinics in the United States to learn as much as I could about their modus operandi. I began to attend the annual meetings of the Academy of Medical Directors to listen and learn. We began to recruit surgeons to broaden our services. We established general and urologic surgery, and began to look for a Cardiovascular surgeon. In the medical field, we added dermatology and rheumatology and additional Cardiologists. Our patients were delighted, but the Valley Baptist Hospital and a significant segment of the medical community had serious concerns over our long-term goals and the potential portion of the medical arena that might accrue to such a large group. Some physicians in the community rumored that referrals sent to us were not sent back to the referring physician until circulated within our own specialists. This was an evil accusation designed to damage our integrity because that simply did not happen.

When cardiac catheterization evolved certain elements in the community tried to block one of our invasive Cardiologists from privileges in the catheter lab claiming him to be incompetent. We brought in the Houston Cardiologist who wrote the book on heart catheterization, and he reviewed seventeen of the accused doctor's cases and declared our man to be "a better than average invasive cardiologist". Today that Cardiologist is recognized as one of the best in his field. Such were the shenanigans of those motivated by greed and fear. One thing was becoming very clear. Valley Diagnostic Clinic Chairman John Ferris, M.D. was not going to suffer any more abuse from liaisons between the hospital and the independents of the community. I encouraged the group to hire a very prominent anti-trust lawyer from Washington D.C. to evaluate our situation and see if we had a case against Valley Baptist Hospital for its collusion with its independents to stop our efforts to achieve our goal of becoming a large multidisciplinary clinic to serve our patients more comprehensively. Indeed, we had a case and this attorney was willing to take the case 'pro bono' he was so sure he could win. We did pay him $20,000 for his initial studies but from there we would have had no appreciable costs.

At that time I had a serious family emergency that took me out of town for several days, and when I returned, I had been recalled and was no longer chairman of the Valley Diagnostic Clinic. I'm not so sure that my recall was legal, but I didn't care. I no longer wished to be associated with a group that chose to act when I was out of town and vulnerable. Actually I couldn't believe what they did, and I couldn't wait to leave the clinic. A few years thereafter they suffered their certain demise and went their separate ways.

When I left the group, I called Dr. Max Harris and asked him if I could come over and occupy half of his office since a woman internist that he was associated with had moved out. He was kind enough to allow me the privilege of moving in with him and that gave me a practice location. Max retired 10 months later after selling his building to the Valley Baptist Hospital. Dr. Harris has remained active up to this time with the Valley Baptist Board of Trustees and the Heinrich and Annie Lamm Memorial and Medical Staff Trust Fund. He has been a most gracious and supportive friend to me.

As the saying goes, "Old doctors don't have to retire – their patients will retire them." And surely that has happened to me. After 55 and a half years, the attrition of my patient population became so acute that I was having to put $1,000 – $2,000 a month into the kitty just to stay open. I made a last stand in the office of Dr. Ruben Lopez, Cardiovascular Surgeon, when he offered me office space at any price I felt I could afford. How generous and respectful is that? There were no strings attached. I managed to make it nine months more but then still couldn't make ends meet and had to retire from private practice. I shall never forget the concern and situation of this fine man and his wife, Adriana, who was so kind to Sarah and me.

For about thirteen years, I had been taking night and occasional weekend call at the Rio Grand State Center in Harlingen. This state sponsored institution handled acute psychiatric emergencies with a separate division for mental retardation. I have truly enjoyed my work there. When Dr. O'Donnell took a position with the State

Prison System, I worked half days taking his place on an hourly basis. I liked the work so well, I applied for the full time position vacated by Dr. O'Donnell and was hired as a Level III clinician for the Mental Retardation Unit. I have a wonderful nurse to work with in the person of Belinda Randle, who has taught me so much about the residents there and the system of care. We have an administrative assistant in the person of Kendra Cookingham, who is bright and alert and helps us with our records and appointments. I believe we are a great team and that makes our work a joy rather than a chore.

Another great feature of my new position is a fellow physician, Dr. Jonathan Yamaguchi, who is in charge of the medical care of the clients in the psychiatric division of the hospital. He has been with the system for about 20 years and is very up-to-date clinically. He is very helpful to me as I navigate these uncharted waters. I really respect his clinical acumen and his fellowship in keeping our respective populations healthy.

So, things change and we must adapt or die on the vine. I have been very good at adaptation and hope to continue to be so. I am now 86 years of age (only 21 and a half in Leap Years) and still have a strong desire to make my life count for as much as possible on this earth. My wife of more than 61 years Sarah has given us ten wonderful children, who returned the favor by giving us 38 grandchildren, and 2 great grandchildren and 2 more greats by Billy Adams' marriage to Kelli. We are so blessed. I have a good friend who is happily married to a wonderful woman, but often laments that he has no children or family of his own with whom to relate in his waning years. It seems to be the only sadness in his life.

Just tonight as I write this story, we received a call from our grandson, John A. Ferris, IV to inform us that he and Heather are expecting their second daughter in September, and that she will be named Sarah. We are so pleased and so proud of that young family and their courage in defending our nation as members of the U.S. Air Force. John IV has had two tours in the Middle East and is currently teaching young pilots the secrets of the F-15.

One aspect of our life that I haven't covered is the time Sarah and I spent in agriculture and the marketing of our crops. I did speak earlier of our friendship with Howard Lievens and his wife Betty. They had eight children who were peers of our group. We loved to be with them during holidays and at Spring harvest time when the roastin' ears of corn were so succulent, dressed with fresh tomatoes, 1015 onions and watermelons for dessert. We often saw and gathered with the J.R. Wade family and their eight children, and occasionally Jerry and Caroline MacManus and their large group of children. Those four Catholic families, with 4 dads and 4 moms, with God's help gave birth to 34 wonderful children who loved each other and loved the land we lived in. Sadly, the Wades would lose their son, John, and the Lievens would lose their John, both in agricultural-related accidents. Sarah and I believe, as do many others, there is no greater pain than the loss of a child. Though we have not personally experienced such grief, we have been close enough to also feel the pain. I heard the news about John Lievens in the middle of a busy afternoon appointment schedule. I dropped everything and drove to the Lievens' farm as fast as I safely could and put my arm around my dear friend and wept with him to empty our sorrow into the loving Hands of Our Lord and Savior, Jesus Christ.

Recently I was in the La Feria area for a hair cut with my patient and dear friend Carolyn Vargas. She also helps Sarah from time to time. Many times I will just drive around and look at my old office and our old home, which has really been spruced up by Mr. and Mrs. Steve Brewer. On this occasion I had a little more time than usual, so I drove out to the old La Feria Cemetery and walked among the graves to see where some of my former patients lay and relived my relationship with them and their families as a very young country doctor. I found John Lievens grave and prayed for him and Howard, and asked if he could ask the Lord to protect and help all of us to live better and stronger lives and love one another by burying all the anguish we generate amongst ourselves.

Sarah and I loved our life in the Valley so much we wanted the agricultural opportunities surrounding us to become more a part of our family life. Every time I had the money and the chance, I would acquire a 10 or 15 acre block of land surrounding the west side of Stuart Place Road and the west side of Russell Lane. We farmed that land while the area matured and its value increased. I was introduced to my good friend Charlie Wetegrove from Raymondville, where he and his sons farmed and operated a produce shed to market Valley produce. Charlie's specialty was onions, and he shipped many a ton to the eastern markets. Charlie thought he knew where every onion plant in the Valley was located, and he would drive around on Sunday mornings and check the vital signs of every onion patch from Brownsville to Rio Grande City. When my 60 acre crop of 1015's was about ready, I called my banker Dave Rogers, who also packed and shipped onions, to come look them over and get ready for the harvest. I was appropriately shocked when he informed me that his shed no longer shipped U.S. onions and was receiving all their produce from Mexico. My heart skipped a few beats as I thought about my farm loan and its dependence on the success of this beautiful onion crop. Dave said he would talk to Charlie Wetegrove who might be able to harvest and ship this beautiful crop of 1015 onions. Charlie didn't waste any time coming to see an onion field that he didn't know existed. It was just across from the Harlingen Country Club on North Stuart Place Road. He was surprised! He and his boys harvested and marketed those onions, and I received a fat check and a fast friendship was formed with the Wetegrove family. Charlie would pick me up at the house every Sunday morning, and we'd have breakfast and then tour many onion fields in the Rio Grande Valley. He taught me so much about farming and Ag related business. Charlie and I remained fast friends until the day

128

he passed away. I attended his funeral, paid my respects and offered my prayers for the repose of his soul and the peace of mind of his dear wife, Irene. She and Charlie also had ten children and the bond of raising a large family enriched our friendship. Our lives have been so much richer because of our friends and contacts outside the cocoon of medicine.

At this juncture I would like to speak of a dear circle of friends who have meant so much to Sarah and me. They were Tommy and Margie Mayfield, Bert and Doris DuBois and Charlie and Patsy Winn. This small group has gathered so many times at the Winn Lodge on the Laureles Division of the King Ranch just out side of Corpus Christi, or at the Winn vacation home at River Ridge on the Bandera Highway at the southern edge of Kerrville. Tommy and Margie went to Texas A & I where they met, fell in love and married. I never met a man that I revered any more than Tommy. His warmth and hospitality made Sarah and me feel so welcome when we visited in their home. He was extremely intelligent, and his success in the farming and cattle business was legend. When Tommy talked with a person that individual would feel that he was the best friend that Tommy ever had. Margie was just a perfect life partner for Tommy and the two of them had a capacity to love their friends no matter what befell them.

Sarah and I bought a 96-acre farm from them and we put it all into citrus. We had 5 acres of Meyer lemons that came off the tree in August, early Marrs oranges that came off in September, navel oranges that took us through November and December, Rio Red grapefruit from November through March, and Valencia oranges that were superb in February. It took five lean years to get those trees into commercially viable production, and I know there were moments when Tommy and Margie were holding their breath and wondering if we would make it. We marketed our fruit through two roadside stores and a gift shipping company known as Ferris Valley Groves that shipped to every state in the Union. Life was good, and Sarah was very active in promoting and keeping an eye toward our business. The story had a glorious ending when we sold our farm and paid Tommy and Margie and sold our gift shipping company to Crockett Farms who still ship under the name of Ferris Valley Groves. Tommy passed away recently after a losing battle with Multiple Myeloma. I never saw anyone fight any harder to defeat that cruel disease. We miss him dearly and show as much love as we can to support Margie in her grief.

Bert DuBois is a lovable retired insurance man who strums and sings many old favorites of our generation to the delight of the rest of us. He tolerates my singing along side of him and that makes me really have a good time because I love music. Bert raises cattle as a pastime and tells one misogynous joke after another relating to the marital state. He wouldn't be alive today if Doris wasn't an understanding and forgiving woman. Bert loves to play poker and will always be in the winner's circle. Doris is a fun loving extrovert who has recently been challenged by her own battle with cancer. After surgery and chemotherapy, she has been declared free of any signs of tumor. This battle has taken an emotional toll on her, and we are all encouraging her to keep up the good fight. We want to see her regain her fun loving personality and be the life of our reunions. I've talked a great deal about Charlie Winn, and I dearly love this strong gentleman whose life has been an example of courage and leadership and the willingness to assume calculated risks to make the world a better place for everyone. Only his strong faith in God has guided and blessed his efforts to be a major contributor to the oil & gas industry. I believe his greatest talent has been that of peacemaker. His solution to any of the problems experienced by mankind is to communicate, talk and keep talking until differences are resolved. For Charlie, this axiom holds true whether it's family, business, or geopolitical.

Charlie had a long relationship with President George H. W. Bush and often had him and Secretary James Baker as guests at the Winn Lodge for quail hunting. I was privileged to be invited to several of those hunts and came to be a frequent correspondent with the President. He loved our grapefruit and always wrote and thanked me for remembering him and the First Lady. He was particularly happy when I would bring enough grapefruit for the Secret Service agents to take home with them. This President was very respectful of the men who volunteered to put their lives between him and harm's way.

He told me that the greatest sorrow of his life was the loss of his two crew members when their torpedo bomber was hit by hostile fire as they made a bombing run over Tinian Island. The President gave the order to eject the disabled aircraft, and he parachuted into the sea. He never saw those two men again. Through the grace of God, a courageous submarine captain observed these events through his periscope, surfaced and rescued our future President before the pursuing Japanese PT boats could get to him.

On one of these quail hunts, Charlie permitted me to invite my grandson, John A. Ferris, IV, who was then Adjutant Commander of the Corps and a senior at Texas A & M. This was a thrilling visit for this young man who had already decided to pursue a career in the regular Air Force and make it his vocation. He called a few days ago to tell Mamaw that he and his wife, Heather, are expecting their 2nd daughter in September and will be naming her Sarah. Mamaw is so pleased, and so am I.

As the saying goes, "Behind every great man one will find a woman whose steadfastness, inner strength, loving heart and strong belief in the teachings of Jesus Christ, are the guarantors of his worldly success." That surely is Patsy Winn. On evenings together after the dinner dishes are put away, we gather for final thoughts of the day and you can find Charlie curled up like a baby in Patsy's arms. A place from whence comes his immense strength as a man of the world.

All good things must come to an end, but one way to prolong a story that is more enduring than one's memory is to record it for posterity. That is what I have tried to do in this book. This effort will mean little to many and a great deal to a few. To those few, I dedicate this work with my deepest appreciation and love for all of you. May the Lord keep you securely in the palm of His wounded hand now and forever. Amen.